Leslie R. James

Toward an Ecumenical Liberation Theology

A Critical Exploration of Common Dimensions in the Theologies of Juan L. Segundo and Rubem A. Alves

PETER LANG
New York • Washington, D.C./Baltimore • Bern
Frankfurt am Main • Berlin • Brussels • Vienna • Oxford

BT
83.57
.J35
2001

Library of Congress Cataloging-in-Publication Data

James, Leslie R.
Toward an ecumenical liberation theology: a critical
exploration of common dimensions in the theologies
of Juan L. Segundo and Rubem A. Alves / Leslie R. James.
p. cm. — (American university studies. VII, Theology and religion; vol. 194)
Includes bibliographical references and index.
1. Liberation theology—History of doctrines. 2. Segundo, Juan Luis—
Contributions in liberation theology. 3. Alves, Rubem A., 1933–   —
Contributions in liberation theology. I. Title. II. Series: American
university studies. Series VII, Theology and religion; vol. 194.
BT83.57.J35   230'.0464—dc21   98-42954
ISBN 0-8204-3345-4
ISSN 0740-0446

Die Deutsche Bibliothek-CIP-Einheitsaufnahme

James, Leslie R.:
Toward an ecumenical liberation theology: a critical
exploration of common dimensions in the theologies
of Juan L. Segundo and Rubem A. Alves /Leslie R. James.
–New York; Washington, D.C./Baltimore; Bern; Frankfurt
am Main; Berlin; Brussels; Vienna; Oxford: Lang.
(American university studies: Ser. 7, Theology and religion; Vol. 194)
ISBN 0-8204-3345-4

The paper in this book meets the guidelines for permanence and durability
of the Committee on Production Guidelines for Book Longevity
of the Council of Library Resources.

Printed in the United States of America

Toward an Ecumenical Liberation Theology

American University Studies

Series VII
Theology and Religion

Vol. 194

PETER LANG
New York • Washington, D.C./Baltimore • Bern
Frankfurt am Main • Berlin • Brussels • Vienna • Oxford

In Memory of

Wilfred T. and Ismay James
Eugene P. Benjamin
H. Dillon and Marjorie Baptiste

With Love and Gratitude for the grace encountered in you.

Acknowledgments

This completed study was begun with the gracious assistance and contributions of many persons which are hereby acknowledged. I wish to express my appreciation to Professors Henry Charles, Bernhard Asen and Ronald Modras who directed this study in its dissertation phase. Special thanks to Dr. Henry Charles, formerly of Saint Louis University, for his invaluable suggestions and continued assistance in the further development of this work. Appreciation is also expressed to Saint Louis University and its Department of Theological Studies for their contribution toward the earlier stage of this work. Thanks also to DePauw University and its President, Dr. Robert Bottoms, for providing needed financial support toward the completion of this work. I am also grateful for the encouragement of Professor Bernard F. Batto, and formerly Chair of the Department of Religious Study, DePauw University. Thanks to Peter Lang Publishing, Inc. I am grateful to Dr. Heidi Burns, Senior Editor, for the encouragement and continued interest she showed in seeing this project completed. Thanks to members of the production staff who had oversight of this project at various stages. Thanks to Janice Harbaugh, for the secretarial assistance she rendered in the initial stages of typing. I owe a tremendous debt of gratitude to Theresa Noble for typing the final draft of this work. My hope is that she derived some measure of joy as she worked on this project. In the final analysis, I am absolutely responsible for any errors.

Thanks to Stephanie Aban and Sandra James, my sisters, who helped in various ways as I sought to bring this project to life. Thanks to all my students; especially those at DePauw University who have awaited the publication of this work. Thanks to my friends in the Greencastle community for their encouragement in this project. With deepest gratitude I acknowledge the devotion of Caroline, my wife, and Leslie-Ann, our daughter, who kept me working on this assignment. They share the dedication of this work along with my father-in-law, Eugene Pitman Benjamin, who unfortunately joined the ancestors before holding the text in hand. The new millennium will confront humankind with new ways of knowing and being. An essential task of religion, as an academic discipline and praxis, will involve mapping visions of communal existence through which human beings can transcend their particularities in forging a new humanity. I continue to be excited over the ways in which Liberation Theology has opened avenues for peace, reconciliation, and the humanization of so many areas of human enterprise. I trust that this study has contributed to an emerging culture of peace and reconciliation.

I would also like to thank the following publishers for permission to reprint from the following works:

A Theology of Human Hope by Rubem A. Alves, 1969 reprinted in 1975, Abby Press, St. Meinrad, Indiana.

Theology and Critical Theory: The Discourse of the Church by Paul Lakeland, 1990, Abington Press, Nashville, Tennessee.

Amnesty of Grace: Justification by Faith from a Latin American Perspective by Elsa Támez, 1993, Abingdon Press, Nashville, Tennessee.

I Believe in the Resurrection of the Body by Rubem A. Alves, 1986, Augsburg Fortress Publishers, Minneapolis, Minnesota.

Church, Charism & Power: Liberation Theology and the Institutional Church by Leonardo Boff, 1985, The Crossroad Publishing Company, New York, New York.

Liberating Reformed Theology: A South African Contribution to an Ecumenical Debate by John W. de Gruchy, 1991, Wm. B. Eerdmans Publishing Company, Grand Rapids, Michigan.

Tomorrow's Child by Rubem A. Alves, 1972, Harper Collins Publishers, New York, New York.

Theology of Hope by Jürgen Moltman, 1967, Harper Collins Publishers, New York, New York.

Theology of the Church by Juan Luis Segundo, 1985, Harper Collins Publishers, New York, New York.

Vatican Council II: The Conciliar and Post-Conciliar Documents, 1980, (Fifth Printing), Austin Flannery, editor, Liturgical Press, Collegeville, Minnesota.

Protestantism and Repression: A Brazilian Case Study by Rubem A. Alves, 1985, Orbis Books, Maryknoll, New York.

What is Religion? by Rubem A. Alves, 1984, Orbis Books, Maryknoll, New York.

Liberating Grace by Leonardo Boff, 1979, Orbis Books, Maryknoll, New York.

The Christ of the Ignatian Exercises by Juan Luis Segundo (trans. John Drury), 1987, Orbis Books, Maryknoll, New York.

The Community Called Church by Juan Luis Segundo, 1973, Orbis Books, Maryknoll, New York.

Grace and the Human Condition by Juan Luis Segundo (trans. John Drury), 1973, Orbis Books, Maryknoll, New York.

The Liberation of Theology by Juan Luis Segundo, 1976, Orbis Books, Maryknoll, New York.

The Sacraments Today by Juan Luis Segundo (trans. John Drury), 1974, Orbis Books, Maryknoll, New York.

The Challenge of the Basic Christian Community edited by Sergio Torres and John Eagleson (trans. John Drury), 1980, Orbis Books, Maryknoll, New York.

Church, Charism & Power: Liberation Theology and the Institutional Church by Leonardo Boff, 1985, SCM Press Ltd, London, England.

Nature and Grace: Dilemmas in the Modern Church by Karl Rahner, S.J., 1964, Sheed & Ward, New York, New York.

Theology of the Reformers by Timothy George, The Sunday School Board, Nashville, Tennessee.

The Absolute Value of Human Action by Frances Stefano, 1992, University Press of America, Lanham, Maryland.

Table of Contents

Preface

Liberation Theology has been the subject of study and commentary from a variety of perspectives. There is little doubt that ecumenism as envisioned by Roman Catholics and Protestants, particularly in the wake of Vatican II, no longer widely ignites the ecclesial imagination. Prevailing ecumenical currents, as Robert Wuthnow observed in *The Restructuring of American Religion*, are more oriented to controversial socio-moral issues: gay rights, women in the priesthood, abortion and euthanasia.

This book returns ecumenism to theology and theological debate. This alone would make it an achievement of value. But the author intends more. His conviction is that Liberation Theology is the only contemporary theological (re)construction that goes beyond the Reformation and Counter-Reformation.

Liberation theologians of both communions agree. It is striking to note how from the beginning, unknown to one another, a convergence in their work occurred around the same emphases: that theology had to transcend the old distinctions between grace and nature, and situate Scripture, sacraments, and Christian discipleship firmly within the struggles of the historical arena. This is Juan Luis Segundo speaking for the Roman Catholics:

> As I experienced the birth of a new Latin American theology, it was something like a spontaneous generation of a common thought arising in isolation in various parts of the continent. Only when various Latin American (by birth or by adoption) theologians began to meet and share the views of one another did we begin to perceive similarities and differences.[1]

And Rubem Alves for the Protestant side:

> My theological explorations are thus intended to be nothing more than an expression of participation in a community of Christians who are struggling to discover how to speak faithfully the language of faith in the context of their commitment to the historical liberation of man.[2]

Segundo and Alves, the author's representative theologians, are, despite differences in style, theme, and personal vocabulary, excellent examples of the growing rapprochement that Liberation Theology describes. The human vocation to liberation is essentially a convocation; transcendence and salvation are continuous and discontinuous with human history; ecclesiology and sacramentology require active commitment to real personal and social transformation; the spiritual life is an integral life, a unity of the temporal and the eternal.

Liberation Theology as ecumenical theology deserves more attention. The author has provided an excellent introduction to a dimension of contemporary theology which is fresh, vital and hopeful.

Henry J. Charles, Ph.D.
Washington, DC

Notes

[1]Juan Luis Segundo, *Theology and the Church: A Response to Cardinal Ratzinger and a Warning to the Whole Church.* Trans. John W. Dierckmeier. San Francisco: Harper, 1987, p. 74.

Chapter 1

Medellín, Liberation Theology, and Common Christian Origins

Latin American Liberation Theology is perhaps the most dramatic expression of the significance of history and experience in post-Vatican II Roman Catholic theology. It has offered a way of doing theology that begins, develops and culminates in a response to the variety of destructive experiences that plague human life—oppression, marginalization, injustice, hunger, and persecution. Since 1968, with the endorsement of the Latin American Bishops at Medellín, Colombia, Liberation Theology has "gone into all the world."[1] It has had an immeasurable impact on Feminist theology, Black Theology, Third World theologians, and on the official language, positions and policies of churches everywhere.

The emphasis on social transformation and the privileged status of the poor are some of the most widely acknowledged features of Liberation Theology in Latin America, but the movement represents much more.

At Medellín the Latin American Bishops met to situate Vatican II's ecclesiological vision within the pastoral situation of Latin America. The title of the official documents indicates the function the Bishops felt the Church had to play in the contemporary history of Latin America: "The Church in the Present-Day Transformation of Latin America in the Light of the Council."[2]

Reading the "*signs of the times*"[53] on the continent, the Bishops spoke of the first indications of the painful birth of a new civilization, under the dynamism of the Holy Spirit.[4] The vision of the Bishops extended not only to Latin America but an implied thrust towards the whole "*Oikoumene,*"[5] all humankind across all temporal boundaries." Implicit also was a theology of grace in which divine presence and human initiative were united and not opposed. Medellín also spoke explicitly of ecumenical activity, in terms of the common vocation of Christian and non-

Christian communities to collaboration in "this fundamental task of our times."[6]

Different theologians subsequently underlined the early historic liberationist response of Christians on the continent to this vocation. Leonardo Boff wrote of the commitment of Christian groups to rescue faith in Latin America from the cynicism that traditionally accompanied belief.[7] Leonardo and Clodovis Boff referred to the origins of Liberation Theology in independent and courageous thinking and in wide-ranging dialogues between Roman Catholic and Protestant theologians.

Juan Luis Segundo provided perhaps the clearest statement of the common roots of Liberation Theology:

> As I experienced the birth of a new Latin American theology, it was something like a spontaneous generation of a common thought arising in isolation in various parts of the continent.Only when various Latin American (by birth or by adoption) theologians began to meet and share the views of one another did we begin to perceive similarities and convergences. Segundo's reference to similarities and convergences indicates what has become a way to describe the liberation theological thrust in Latin America: not a school, but a movement, comprising a wide spectrum of theologians, with distinctive approaches but with concerns bearing fundamental family resemblances.

Among the major Roman Catholic contributors are: Gustavo Gutiérrez-Merino, Hugo Assmann, Leonardo Boff, José Porfirio Miranda, Juan Luis Segundo, and Jon S. Sobrino. Protestant liberation theologians include: Rubem A. Alves, José Míguez-Bonino, and Elsa Támez. Thomas Hanks is also an important evangelical voice.

The Roman Catholic Range

Gustavo Gutiérrez-Merino (b. 1928), a widely respected theologian throughout the world, is the Dean and patriarchal figure among liberation theologians. His classic work, *A Theology of Liberation*, is widely regarded as a foundational text in Liberation Theology.

Hugo Assmann (b. 1933) studied sociology and philosophy in Brazil, and theology in Rome. His best-known work is *Theology for a Nomad Church* (Orbis Books, 1976). Assmann is considered an excellent synthesizer of liberation themes. He stresses the need for a new theological language—from him comes the phrase "the epistemological privilege of the poor." His use of social sciences includes an explicit critique of the Marxist overemphasis on economics.

Leonardo Boff (b. 1938) studied theology and philosophy at Curitiba and Petropolis in Brazil. He received his doctorate at Munich. He also studied at Oxford, Louvain, and Würzburg. Boff's most famous work is perhaps *Church: Charism and Power. Liberation Theology and the Institutional Church* (Trans. John W. Diercksmeier, Crossroad, 1988). This is fundamentally a work in liberation ecclesiology in which the poor re-invent the Church (ecclesiogenesis). Boff has also contributed to Christology from a liberationist perspective. His important work in this regard is *Jesus Christ as Liberator: A Critical Christology for Our Time* (Orbis, 1978).

José Porfirio Miranda. Born in Mexico, Miranda studied economics at Munich and Münster. He also did biblical studies at the Biblical Institute in Rome. Miranda has focused on highlighting the affinities between Marxism and the Bible. This constitutes the substance of his *Marx and the Bible: A Critique of the Philosophy of Oppression* (Orbis, 1974). Miranda is no Marxist ideologue. He criticizes both interpretations of Marx and of Christ, but he remains essentially linked to establishing correlations between Marxism and the Christian faith.

Jon S. Sobrino. Born in Spain, Sobrino studied mechanical engineering at Saint Louis University, and theology at the Hochschule Sankt Georgen, Frankfurt. Sobrino's interests include Christology. He sees the contemporary Latin American situation as similar to Palestine in the time of Jesus. His major work is perhaps *Christology at the Crossroads: A Latin American Approach* (Orbis, 1978).

Juan Luis Segundo (b. 1925). Segundo is the most prolific of Latin American liberation theologians. He studied philosophy in Argentina, and theology at Louvain, Belgium, and at the University of Paris. Segundo is the theologian who represents the Roman Catholic perspective for purposes of this study. While Gutiérrez is the acknowledged father of the movement in Latin America, Segundo is the thinker with the greater system, definition of method, and theological and ecclesiological expansiveness. The following summary gives some indication of the range of his theology and his system:

(a) Theology is reflection on the real life experience of ordinary believers.
(b) Theology critiques the magical or bank-deposit notion of the sacraments.
(c) Segundo places greater emphasis on the methodology over against the content of Liberation Theology. He is the liberation theologian

who has explicitly developed a liberation methodology—the hermeneutical circle.

(d) Ecclesiologically, Segundo advocates the notion of the Church as a heroic minority, criticizing the integrity of much pastoral practice and the nature of the Church of Christendom. For Segundo, only a minority Church can be efficacious in history.

(e) "Faith," Segundo argues, "is never without ideologies," and "ideology without faith is never an ideology.[8]

(f) Of great significance to Segundo is the divorce between faith and history. Segundo's theology is essentially a liberationist theology of grace attempting to transcend this dichotomy.

The Protestant Range

José Míguez-Bonino (b. 1924), a Methodist, studied at the Evangelical Theologate in Buenos Aires, Argentina, Emory University, and Union Theological Seminary in the United States of America. He has been a President of the World Council of Churches and was a Protestant observer at Vatican II. Bonino's book, *Doing Theology in a Revolutionary Situation* (Fortress Press, 1975) is a seminal contribution to Liberation Theology. In this work, theology arises out of the experience of oppression in the light of biblical faith. The notion of the hermeneutical circle is implicit in this book. The circle completes a process of liberative reflection in which there is a struggle for totality in the face of dehumanization and fragmented existence.

Elsa Támez is a professor of Biblical Studies at the Seminario Latinoamericano, San José, Costa Rica. Támez' focus is the development of a biblical hermeneutic for the oppressed of Latin America. She also brings to the liberation agenda a critique of sexist *machismo*.

Thomas Hanks is an evangelical theologian, and a graduate of Wheaton Graduate School of Theology. He went to Costa Rica in 1963 as a representative of Intervarsity. His conversion to Liberation Theology stemmed from his exposure to the poverty he saw there. His works include *God So Loved the Third World: The Biblical Vocabulary of Oppression* (Orbis, 1983). Hanks re-discovered the Bible (and biblical inerrancy) in the lived engagement of faith with situations of oppression.

Rubem A. Alves (b. 1933). Alves comes out of the Presbyterian tradition. Alves is to Protestant what Gutiérrez is to Catholic liberationists. Alves was one of the vanguard members in the initial conversations between Protestant and Roman Catholic theologians mentioned earlier by

Segundo and Boff. Alves' distinctive contribution is elaborated via the European theology of hope. His theology has a clear humanist thrust. It responds to the question: What does it take to make and keep human life human? Alves then seeks to harmonize human aspirations and divine activity in a "messianic humanism," and a unified conception of history. Alves is the representative Protestant voice in this study. As we will see, he and Segundo have significant areas of similarity and differences.

Liberation Theology as an Ecumenical Theology

Liberation Theology, as a common thrust among Latin American theologians, represents a theological movement with a vital ecumenical dynamic. As Míguez- Bonino put it, a basic motivation in Liberation Theology is the quest that "prompted the great thinkers of the past to grapple with the dialectical relation of the City of Man and the City of God (Augustine), natural and divine law (Aquinas), civil and Christian righteousness (Luther), common and saving grace (Calvin).[9] After Vatican II, and particularly in the light of its document on Ecumenism, *Unitatis Redintegratio*, the churches of the industrialized First World witnessed an extensive upsurge of national, regional and international meetings and consultations devoted to ecumenism.[10] But three significant differences come to mind between the import of these initiatives and the thrust of Liberation Theology since 1968. First, the results of the nearly thirty years of dialogue between scholars remain still largely unknown to the laity and clergy of the respective denominations or churches. At the ground level ecumenism has hardly begun.[11] Secondly, there is the frank acknowledgment that the movement has in more recent times lost its earlier momentum. "More and more," wrote George S. Lindbeck, a pioneer in Lutheran-Catholic dialogue, and one of the Protestant observers at the Council, "I find myself agreeing that the dialogue is of little current significance either to the organized churches or to movements of renewal . . . The *avant garde* activists and theological progressives are even less concerned."[12] Thirdly, religious or theological ecumenism is increasingly being displaced by secular ecumenism, or by what can be described in Robert Wuthnow's terms as an ecumenism of "special purposes groups."[13] Different groups from different churches and denominations find common cause in positions on highly controversial socio-moral issues. Such mergers have little to do with traditional differences in religious affiliation.

The ecumenical dynamic in Liberation Theology by contrast remains both deeply theological as well as fundamentally rooted and engaged with issues of great social significance. In theological expression, indeed, Liberation Theology can perhaps be said, as Bonino implied, to be the only contemporary theological school of re-construction that goes beyond the divides of the Reformation and Counter- Reformation. This is not to claim, of course, that Liberation Theology, is not heir to historical, theological and ecclesiological developments within each communion. It is to say that a vital ecumenical dynamic is at work in this movement as perhaps nowhere else in contemporary church history. The ecumenical dimension, however, is not often adverted to and has been little studied and explored. This study's reflection on that dimension hopefully makes a contribution to that end.

Organization of the Study

Apart from this introductory chapter, the book is organized around four fundamental dimensions of ecclesiological life, that is, grace, faith, ecclesiology itself, and sacraments (inclusive of spirituality). In each of these areas I proceed first with a contrast between the inherited theological configuration, Roman Catholic and Protestant, and the perspective of Liberation Theology. This is followed by an exploration of the area/dimension in Segundo and in Alves, which shows how in these representative thinkers a strong ecumenical convergence of thought and vision is generated.

In Chapter Two, the subject is the dialectic of grace and history. The history of the theological divide on the issue of grace is presumed a theoretical framework of grace and nature. In contemporary Roman Catholic and Protestant theology, the grace/nature relation has progressively given way to a dialectical relation of grace and history, or more accurately, of grace, history, and eschatology. This theological interrelation, taken up substantively and methodologically in Liberation Theology, has meant a revaluation of human, historical activity; salvation has intrinsic connections to the human, historical task. The Kingdom of God, which the Church serves, is mediated by the praxis of a committed faith. Grace is thus an enabling power, giving birth to a faith which is transformative and does justice. It creates a history of divine-human love and freedom (Segundo), and/or a messianic humanism (Alves). Grace is also present wherever fruits of this freedom, love, and humanism (Kingdom values and activity) are present. Thus ecumenicity also moves from within the Christian communion to embrace in solidarity all who work for the upbuilding of the Kingdom.

Chapter Three follows through on the treatment of the grace-history dialectic by focusing on further implications of transformative faith. What is explored here is a fuller exposition of the way in which Liberation Theology reconceptualizes the interrelation of faith, justification, and sanctification, as integral salvation, within the framework of history and eschatology. In Segundo transformative faith is explored further as freedom from the captivity of Christendom; as making all ideologies relative, and as keeping the hermeneutic circle open and generative. In Alves, building on the Reformed legacy of Calvin's humanism, transformative faith is explored as being creative of history and as making alternative futures possible.

The focus of Chapter Four is on the new lines of ecumenical ecclesiology. Both the Roman Catholic and Protestant churches have revised and modified the historic communitarian character of their ecclesiologies. In the former, the Church as the hierarchical "perfect society" has given way to the Church as a pilgrim, eschatological community, the People of God. In the latter, the Church as a holy community, a priesthood of all believers, now includes a lived and active engagement with history.

Liberation Theology in Segundo and Alves retains and amplifies these revisions with further emphases: the Church as a prophetic community living by the logic of the paschal mystery; as the embodiment of messianic creativity; as servant of humankind; as unique, non-mass-produced community; as heroic, minoritarian community.

Chapter Five deals with sacramentology and spirituality. With respect to the sacraments, both Segundo and Alves situate the reality and power of sacramental signification within a historical-eschatological perspective. The sacraments are thus not only signs of (different aspects of) liberation but of eschatological anticipation, aperitifs of the Kingdom, as Alves describes them. They are also the communitarian fashioning of the Church and its pedagogy for mission. In this area, too, because of the overarching framework of history-eschatology, classic theological differences now appear as variations on a common theme rather than totally discordant conceptions.

In spirituality, important implications follow from the disappearance of the "two-tiered" universe or the two-story world picture, and the consensus around a unified theory of grace. Catholic spirituality no longer speaks of "spiritual" as opposed to or of more importance and value than "temporal." "Humanization" integrally unites both spheres. In Alves, one can no longer speak of a Protestant "lacuna" where spirituality is concerned. The theology generated by the unified theory of grace gives rise in his reflection, as in Segundo's, to spirituality as a counter-cultural way of commitment, a lived, hopeful vision of an enhanced future, which includes a freedom and carnival of the spirit, as well as prophetic solidarity with the oppressed.

Notes

1   In reference to the Great Commission of Jesus to his disciples in Matthew's Gospel 28: 19–20. For a brief but comprehensive history of the pre-formation, genesis, development and consolidation of Liberation Theology see Roberto Oliveros, "Historia de la Teología de la Liberación," in Ignacio Ellacuría and Jon Sobrino, eds. Mysterium Liberationis: Conceptos Fundamentales de la Teología de la Liberación, I, II. (Madrid: Editorial Trotta, S. A., 1992.), pp. 17–50.

2   See The Documents of CELAM II: (a) Latin American Episcopal Council (CELAM II), *The Church in the Present-Day Transformation of Latin America in the Light of the Council: I Position Papers*. Bogota, D.E., Colombia: General Secretariat of CELAM, 1970) and (b) Second General Conference of Latin American Bishops, *The Church in the Present-Day Transformation of Latin America in the Light of the Council: II Conclusions* (Second Edition), (Washington, D.C.: Division for Latin America-USC, 1973).

3   See Matt. 16:3. This eschatological category, "the signs of the times," was adopted by Vatican II in order for the Church to carry out its mission in the modern world. This adoption was made in the Pastoral Constitution on the Church in the Modern World, *Gaudium et Spes*. As such it determined the new context in which Catholic theology was essentially to be done; a communal-historical/eschatological framework.

4   *The Church in the Present-Day Transformation of Latin America in the Light of the Council: II Conclusions*, p. 35.

5   For a study in the history of the etymology of the term "*Oikoumene*" see William Adolf Visser 't Hooft, "The Word 'Ecumenical'—Its History and Use," in Ruth Rouse and Stephen Charles Neil, *A History of the Ecumenical Movement*, Vol. 1, 1517–1948, Third Edition, (Geneva: World Council of Churches, 1986), pp. 735–40.

6   *The Church in the Present-Day Transformation of Latin America, II. Conclusions*, p. 64.

7   Leonardo Boff, "The Contribution of Liberation Theology to a New Paradigm." in Hans Küng in *Theology: A Symposium for the Future*, trans. Margaret Köhl (New York: Crossroad, 1989), p. 108.

8   Juan Luis Segundo, *Faith and Ideologies*, Volume I of *Jesus of Nazareth Yesterday and Today*, trans. John Drury (Maryknoll, N.Y.: Orbis Books, Victoria: Dove Communications, London: Sheed and Ward, 1984), p. 142.

9   José Míguez-Bonino, *Doing Theology in a Revolutionary Situation*, (Philadelphia: Fortress Press, 1975), xvii.

10   See George Tavard, "Ecumenical Relations," in Adrian Hastings, ed., *Modern Catholicism* (New York: Oxford University Press, 1991). Tavard lists the major dialogues and consultations since 1965 between the Catholic and major Protestant communities directly issued from the Reformation, see p. 417.

11   See George Tavard, Ecumenical Relations," Adrian Hastings, ed., *Modern Catholicism*, p. 420.

12   George Lindbeck, "The Future of the Dialogue: Pluralism or an Eventual Synthesis of Doctrine," in Joséph Papin, ed., *Christian Action and Openness to the World* (Pennsylvania: The Villanova Press, 1970), pp. 38–39.

13   Robert Wuthnow, *The Restructuring of American Religion: Society and Faith Since World War II.* (New Jersey: Princeton University Press, 1988), p. 112, 121–131.

Chapter 2

The Dialectic of Grace and History

Liberation Theology's emphasis on the insertion of grace in history spells a new and significant landmark in the history of grace. The communal and inter-faith consensus on this point clearly signals a theological advance beyond the post-Reformation history of division surrounding the theological meaning of grace. Grace in history means that history and human activity have potentially salvific value; salvation has intrinsic connections to the human historical task. This configuration of grace as a communal and historical-eschatological reality amplifies (and corrects) the traditional theological understanding of grace in individual, ontological and psychological terms. With the traditional emphasis also went a devaluation of all earthly activity, since salvation was a matter of human destiny after death. The insertion of grace in history implies rather a synergistic relation between divine gratuitousness and human co-operation. The building of the Kingdom of God becomes also a project of human commission.

This liberation re-interpretation thus underlines all Christian discipleship as necessarily entailing this historical-eschatological dimension. It envisions a life and commitment of praying and acting that the Kingdom may come on earth as it is in heaven. It is also the locus from which a wider extra-ecclesial post-Reformation ecumenicity is generated, that is, from the solidarity in action of all who work for the upbuilding of God's Kingdom.

Catholic Doctrine on Human Regeneration

Post-Reformation Catholic theology increasingly effected a unified theology of grace by breaking down the separation between the "natural" and "supernatural" realms of existence. A unified theology of history also resulted from this movement. The grace of God, freely given in Jesus Christ, remains necessary for salvation, but the Tridentine feature of human co-operation has been retrieved in a broader way.[1] Salvation—or liberation—referred to a process in which the interaction of divine love and human response makes for the upbuilding of the Kingdom. Grace, in other words, was unified love in action.

Catholic liberationists have appropriated this basic post-Reformation thrust on grace and human activity and inserted it into the social realities of Latin America. Grace here becomes incarnationally the task of building a new Latin American humanity based on the person of Jesus Christ.[2] Catholic liberationists have in fact gone further. The new dialectic has pushed them toward formulating regeneration in cosmic terms.[3] Grace is at work to re-create the entire cosmos, not only either the individual or society. It becomes the principle which continually propels the universe towards increasingly wider forms and realms of unity.[4]

This cosmic emphasis on the end of transformation as eschatological unity, owes, of course, much to the thought of Teilhard de Chardin. In fact, Teilhard's evolutionist categories re-echo as a *leitmotif* throughout Segundo's work. According to James Lyons, what was of primary importance to Teilhard was that the evolving world should have a goal. It was a notion which Teilhard derived not from evolutionary theory, but from Christian eschatology, other Christian sources, Blondel, also, and Scholasticism.

The movement in Catholic theology toward a unified theology of grace and history represents a long history of theological development, of which Liberation Theology is both fruit and climax. First, the formulation of the doctrine of "*natura pura*" represented a wish to preserve the gratuitous quality of grace as God's self-gift. The net result was, however, that a chasm separated nature from grace. Human nature had no strong orientation to the divine order; at best it had only a "lack of repugnance" toward it.[5] Henri de Lubac's *The Mystery of the Supernatural* places these notions of separation and lack of repugnance within the wider context of the history of theology.[6] Dissatisfaction with this understanding led then to an emphasis on a distinction not a separation between the two realms. In human nature there was a real longing for the divine, not simply a lack of repugnance. Some theologians still felt that this detracted from grace's gratuitous character, and proposed that the longing for God was a simple possibility without any significant effect in or on human nature.

Through a return to the thought of Aquinas, a retrieval took place of the idea of an innate human predisposition to know God. Such a predisposition was constitutive of human being. Grace finishes or completes this profound inner human aspiration, and is where human being achieves complete fulfillment. Nature and supernature therefore, far from being hostile, were designed to be intimately related.[7]

As Gutiérrez noted, however, this laudable development still considered grace at a metaphysical, abstract, and essentialist level.[8] Once the inherited dualism was overcome, however, the issue then took a new turn, significantly due to the recovery of the historical and existential points of view. One result of this latter development was Rahner's notion of the "*supernatural existential.*"[9] Whether Catholic theologians today keep or rephrase Rahner's terminology, all agree that the reality it expresses is a matter of common consensus. Thus there has been a progressive emphasis, crystallized at Vatican II, that the term "integral" best represents the way to approach the human vocation.

Lutheran Retrieval and Beyond

Protestant liberationists have retrieved and modified their own inherited tradition in the theology of grace.[10] They have recaptured Luther's basic evangelical thrust: the grace of God is for human liberation. Lutheran doctrine was shaped in response to his subjective, psychological search for a gracious God. Justification by faith in Luther thereafter became formulated in an individual-ontological, nature-grace framework. A dominant result of these developments in Luther was an emphasis on introversion and a certain passive interiority.[11] This is one significant juncture where Protestant liberationists and Luther differ.

The issue for them is not how to find a gracious God but how to end Latin America's history of oppression and disgrace. Their response is neither static nor passive. To end, they contend, Latin American disgrace, grace must historically mediate the transformation of the eschatological future. Elsa Támez succinctly states the difference in perspective:

> One of the principal reasons to approach the theme from a broader perspective is to mark the . . . aspect of social justice that may be in it . . . That step is important if one is to overcome the individualism and subjectivism that permeate the life of faith of the churches, and that prevent the practice of an effective faith. In Latin America the word "liberation" best encompasses or approaches the rereading of justification by faith . . . Certainly justification includes being liberated

by God "from sin, the law, and death"—in all their concrete manifestations—in order to engage oneself without fear in the practice of justice that our peoples need so greatly. The new dimension of this rereading of the doctrine is not in the well known formulation, "freed from . . ., for . . .," which already involves a big step if it is taken seriously. What is novel for us is the consideration of justification and liberation from a historical perspective of oppression, poverty and struggle. In the present moment, the doctrine of justification is being confronted radically by the reality of injustice, whose products are the deaths of thousands of innocent people, and the loss of humanity for thousands more. Those products of injustice constitute the principal challenges of the Latin American reality to a rereading of the doctrine of justification by faith.[12]

The grace that mediates justification is thus an enabling grace, making for an effective, transformative faith, a faith that does justice. Christians are in the process subjects of a potentially alternative history, and co-architects of the Kingdom.

According to Rubem Alves, the Reformation was an attempt to restore to humanity this created dignity. The human being was retrieved in creativity and freedom to be a subject and maker of history:

With its doctrine of "the priesthood of all believers," the Reformation asserted that subjectivity is in direct relationship with the divine. Hence it affirmed the axiological priority of subjective over all institutional crystallizations that stood opposed to it. The human being is divinized, becoming a center of negativity which sets history in motion.[13]

The Reformation originally heard the human cry for freedom and liberation uttered in its day. At the charismatic moment of its appearance, it represented the bursting forth of a repressed cry for freedom

The question is whether Protestantism has preserved its initial vision during the course of its historical evolution.[14]

Human liberation, for Protestant liberationists, is integral to the Christian gospel. While they retrieve the Lutheran insight of grace as liberative, they also generate a theological configuration in which human activity is necessary. Faith, the response to God's initiative to liberate implies a simultaneous commitment to human emancipation.

Extending Calvin's Humanism

Protestant Liberation Theology has also retrieved and reappropriated humanism in the Calvinist tradition.[15] It shares Calvin's passion for the full restoration of the human person. Humanism for Calvin begins with the self-understanding and acknowledgment of human estrangement.[16]

Adam's sin plunged the whole human race into estrangement. God, however, restored fallen humanity through Jesus Christ.[17] The salvific efficacy of Jesus' atonement stemmed not only from the cross, but from his entire life, including his continual ministry of intercession at the Father's right hand.[18]

While Luther emphasized justification, Calvin stressed sanctification.[19] Both are simultaneous gifts arising from union with Christ.[20] The fundamental fact is that we do not belong to ourselves but to the Lord ("*nostri non sumus, sed domini*").[21] In Christ humankind is "*simul et coniunctum in ipso.*" Christ the justifier and sanctifier is the foundation or paradigm for the new eschatological humanity.[22] Through sanctification the new nature emerges daily in the life of the human being, but it remains veiled by sin until death. Human beings will know their full and completely restored humanity in the world to come.[23]

Calvin's stress on sanctification introduced the idea of humanization as processual into Reformation and post-Reformation Protestant theology. Faith for Calvin had a dynamic quality and character. It is this dynamic dimension which has been retrieved by Protestant liberationists. When they insert this humanism into Latin American history, however, they remove it from its grace-nature dialectic and set it more within the communal-historical-eschatological framework already noted. Alves, for instance, who operates out of the Reformed tradition, centers his work around the basic commitment to the human social liberation of persons.[24] His messianic humanism keeps and extends the range of the Calvinist legacy. For Alves, messianic humanism manifests the humanizing determinations of the transcendent. When it names God, it refers to the power that remains committed to set humans free, even when all possibilities in history seem to be exhausted. The name of God is the power that created and keeps creating human beings in freedom.[25]

Mainline Catholic and Protestant liberationists have thus generally gone beyond the post-Reformation legacy on the theology of grace by situating grace within history, and envisioning the relation between divine agency and human response as making possible an alternative history through the praxis of transformed subjects and communities.

Critique of Theologies of Redemption: Redemption as Total Regeneration

The linkage between salvation and history distinguishes Liberation Theology from classical theologies of redemption, which put salvation beyond history. These theologies were partial and a-historical. Salvation did not embrace the totality of human existence in the world, and life in the world was a test of entry into life after death. Liberation critique of these theologies stresses their dualist character, and the fact that in the end they often unwittingly served structures of domination and oppression. By contrast, the idea of salvation for liberationists is total or integral.[26] What grace projects is a total reconfiguration of human existence and history, even as the idea of totality transcends all that humans can achieve in history. Still, history is not bypassed and salvation is not completely outside its realm.

In history a continual struggle takes place with forces that are death-dealing and oppressive. These are forces of the anti-Christ, seeking to subvert the advent of the Kingdom in its plenitude.[42] The ceaseless and pluriform nature of this struggle means that integral salvation has a utopian quality. It is always more than what is present, and more than all temporary defeats and setbacks. Utopia means also that the conversion that integral salvation requires is nothing short of being total and radical. Its vision is one of the complete reconciliation of all things in Christ.

Salvation requires human activity. It is not a passive endowment, but a challenge to liberation and solidarity in the cause of justice. Salvation is an endowment and task, gift and demand. As the Final Document of the International Ecumenical Congress of Theology, Brazil, 1980 put it:

> All people are called by the word of the Gospel, to receive the Kingdom as a gift, to be converted from injustice and from idols to the living and true God, proclaimed by Jesus Christ (Mark 1:15; John 16:3; 1 Thess. 1:9). The Kingdom is grace and must be received as such, but it is also a challenge to new life, to commitment, to liberation and solidarity with the oppressed in the building of a just society. Thus we say that the Kingdom is of God; it is grace and God's work. But at the same time it is a demand and a task for human beings.[28]

Both Segundo and Alves define in different ways the basic emphases of retrieval and amplification so far noted in the inherited understanding of grace. An orthopraxis of the Kingdom can be seen to emerge in their theologies as a converging ecumenism of grace, beyond the traditional historic division and separation.

Grace and History in Segundo

The praxis of creating a history of divine-human love and freedom is the essence of Segundo's theology of grace and history.[29] This theology is a finely elaborated form of the Catholic Latin American reception of Vatican II's "one- tiered" theory of grace.[30] The "one-tiered" theory, which abolished the supernatural-natural divide in post-Tridentine theology, generated a new understanding of existence and a new theology of salvation history (*Heilsgeschichte*).[31] According to Segundo, it opened the way for the new theological paradigm of Liberation Theology.[32] A radical convergence between eternal and temporal values came into being; absolute and transcendental values could be assigned to human action and values.

Segundo recapitulates the history that formed the background to the conciliar adoptions. The background, he says, is the Rahnerian view of pure nature as a "limit concept." All human beings have one vocation, a convocation to one and the same complete supernatural fulfillment. This holds true within and without the Church; the effects of grace within the Christian are the same as those produced by grace in all human beings of goodwill.[33] Grace is everywhere embracing all existence and creation.[34] It is by nature radically ecumenical. As a unifying principle, grace makes all persons potentially active as persons in the paschal mystery of Jesus Christ. Praxis thus makes ecumenicity active and real; it leads all persons and things to their final destiny in Christ. Praxis is grace realized.

The "*one-tiered*" theology endorsed by Vatican II also made possible a rehabilitation of eschatology into post-Vatican II Catholic theology.[35] No longer conceptually confined to being a doctrine of "the last things," eschatology became a vital part of ongoing Christian existence. We live in the light of the coming of the Kingdom, working for and effecting its partial manifestations and alive with longing for greater realizations and ultimate completion. The categories for communicating the efficacy of grace thus shifted from being static, immobilist and essentialist to being active, dynamic, evolutionary and transformative.[36]

Segundo's full-fledged theory of grace is itself the result of an evolution in his own understanding and the fruit of several important contributory influences. These include Scripture, Vatican II, Leopoldo Malevez, Karl Rahner, Teilhard de Chardin, Sigmund Freud, Karl Marx, and of course the Latin American context itself. Segundo's dialogue with these sources led to an evolution in his theology of grace from Malevez's ecumenical understanding of the Council of Orange's interpretation of the "*initium fidei*" to his, that is Segundo's, politicization of Vatican II's theology of grace and history/eschatology. Malevez, his teacher, was a key influence from the start. According to Segundo, the distinctiveness of Malevez's position was that he saw that under the guise of discussions concerning the beginning of faith the issue was really about the human virtues of the pagans. The Fathers had already spoken of such virtues as a preparation for the Gospel. No one, said Malevez, here is prepared for or begins something that totally exceeds his/her possibilities.[537]

Malevez thus anticipated Rahner's more speculative and widely-accepted *Supernatural existential*.[38] Rahner's term conveyed the same meaning expressed by Malevez but did so more explicitly, and with clearer universal dimensions. This development in Catholic theology effectively destroyed the intrinsic dualism in the traditional approach to grace in which the supernatural and the natural were separated.[39] According to Segundo, the theological principle affirmed by the Council of Orange and re-affirmed by Malevez was reiterated by Vatican II's Dogmatic Constitution on the Church (*Lumen Gentium*), when it declared that the Church considers as "a preparation for the Gospel" everything good and true that is found among people who have lived according to their highest potential and in accord with their conscience—even without arriving at explicit knowledge of God.[40]

From Rahner, Segundo, according to José Míguez-Bonino, appropriated the impulse which overcomes the dichotomy of nature and grace by conceiving humankind in its very creaturehood as open to God.[41] From de Chardin he took evolutionary categories which allowed him to reformulate his understanding from an *immobilist* to a *mobilist* framework. Alfred T. Hennelly notes, as did Lyons before him, the crucial importance of Teilhard's writings on Segundo's theological development.[42]

In the light of the foregoing, Segundo was fully prepared to receive and insert Vatican II with its unified theory of grace and history into the cultural specifics of Latin America. Segundo believed that none of the conciliar decrees or constitutions take grace as their theme;[43] the Council's major theme was the Church and her functions.[44] Nevertheless, he felt that "a revitalized vision of the Church presumes an equally revitalized vision of Christian existence and hence of God's gift which is grace."[45]

A further important emendation of Vatican II's theology for Segundo is that the Council's theory of grace was formulated in a context of European presuppositions. To translate the conciliar spirit into the Third World, it was necessary to situate it in terms of Latin America's problems. The hermeneutical principle for this translation is the principle of human applicability. Vatican II underscored this when it emphasized the luminosity of the divine mysteries: the revelation of the Father's love is the revelation of the mystery of human beings and their destiny. Faith enlightens the human being with a new light, which capacitates them to face and solve problems more and more in a humane manner.[46]

Segundo defined the hermeneutical key for interpreting the gospel in Latin America as the *option for the poor*. This is the posture or attitude we adopt, aware of the risk and our responsibility, before the Word of

God, and before reading the Word. We believe that this disposition un-
veils the Word for us. We believe, in the risk of faith, that this is truly what
happens.[47]

The option for the poor represents Segundo's contextualization of
Vatican II's biblical and eschatological category of the "*signs of the times*."
The result was his radical insertion of grace in history and his development of a political understanding of grace that drew further on Scripture,[48] Marx[49] and Freud[50] for interpreting the meaning of integral human salvation.

As a post-Medellín Latin American theologian, Segundo also
contextualizes grace in socio-historical categories.[51] In Latin America grace
in history means a dialectic making for human and historical transformation.[52] Human activity is essential to the dialectic. "The greatest danger
for faith," Segundo observes, "continues to be the divorce between faith
and life with its commitments."[53] Grace and commitment are essentially
related. God's self, which grace communicates, is for human regeneration
and transformation. It is the "great wind that takes hold of our own existence and carries it much further than its innate gravity would permit it to
reach."[54]

For Segundo, Grace—in Marxist terms—overcomes all historical alien
ations.[55] Theologically, it represents a creative-redemptive act of divine-
human co-operation, the divine-human project creating a history of love
in all its fullness. As he put it in *Grace and the Human Condition,* grace
is the irresistible force that seeks to make us free, and turns us toward
others, that we may collaborate in a common work. This work, which is
both human and divine, entails the creation in freedom of a history of
love in all its fullness.[56]

The human response to the irresistibility of grace is faith. Faith leads
then to a liberative praxis of creating a new history of humanization.[57]
Faith in action, the commitment founded on and made possible by grace,
is for Segundo the orthopraxis of the Kingdom.

Alves, the Theology of Hope, and Messianic Humanism

The anthropology that underlies Alves' theology of grace is primarily an
anthropology of human historical freedom.

Today . . . man still oppressed is speaking a different language. It is a language
of his own, which indicates that he has emerged into history. He sees the situation of oppression that dominates him. But his consciousness is no longer domesti-
cated. He is determined to liberate himself historically. In the past, the future was

closed for him and his consciousness was closed to the future. Today, although the future still remains closed, his consciousness is open for the future. He inserts himself into his historical present as a contradiction to it, as a negation which presses toward a new tomorrow. He has become a historical subject with a definite sense of vocation. The new language announces that a new man is born into history.[58]

For Alves humankind and the world are open-ended because in history the possibilities springing from the relations between them are never exhausted. Humans actualize their freedom through action or praxis, through discovering that the world is addressed to them as a horizon into which they can project themselves. When humans respond, the world is different; it ceases to be the isolated sphere of nature and bears the stamp of freedom. Human beings come into being through this exercise of their freedom in action.[59]

Commitment and the praxis of freedom have thus a central place in Alves' theology. They are the "ultimate concern" generating the search for a language that speaks about faith faithfully. Alves' theological explorations are meant to be nothing but a sign of participation in a community of Christians who struggle with the commission of speaking the language of faith faithfully, in the context of their commitment to the historical liberation of human beings.[60]

For Alves the central issue addressed to faith is the question of humanization, that is, Paul Lehmann's question: "What does it take to make and to keep human life human in the world."[61] The language of faith is shaped and influenced by a commitment that mediates this humanization. In the community of faith this humanization is grace. Feuerbach's reduction of theology to anthropology finds a new form in messianic humanism. All God's activity, from start to finish, aims at the liberation of humans."[62]

Grace is present whenever alienations are overcome and humanization is historically mediated. Human activity is thus vital to the presence and effect of grace in the world. For Alves the orthopraxis of humanization is the faithful expression of Christian orthodoxy.

The search for a faithful language to express the commitment of faith, or put differently, to underlie speech about grace, led Alves in his seminal work *A Theology of Human Hope* to address critically Jürgen Moltmann's expression of hope theology in *The Theology of Hope*.[63] Alves' thesis, of course, was itself highly influenced by the hope movement.[64] The criticism he levels against Moltmann is the criticism of an insider.

According to Moltmann, a theology of love was developed in the Middle Ages, and a theology of faith at the time of the Reformation. It is important now, however, to develop a universal theology of hope to prepare and direct the Church, humankind, and nature toward the Kingdom.[65] Hope reconfigures all Christian theology and symbolization. Practically, it embraces the whole of Christian existence, drawing believers into the life of love and freeing them for solidarity with the whole of suffering creation.[66] Alves' fundamental critique of Moltmann is that his theology of hope is not dialectical.[67] It remains tangential to human history. The categories Moltmann uses are also Greek metaphysical, essentialist categories. The theology is thus strongly dualistic and its language fundamentally a-historical. It is not truly liberative because there is no immediacy between the language of hope and the negativity of humankind's present experience in the world.

For Moltmann, the promise creates a new dimension, the *inadequatio rei et intellectus*, that is, it gives the intellect critical distance to negate the present. Human beings, however, feel the pain of the gap between themselves and the world. The *inadequatio rei et intellectus* is a reflection of the inhumanity of the situation which engenders the pain. From this *inadequatio* comes the stretching of consciousness toward such possibilities as would eliminate all the negativity of the present. It is *eros*, Alves concludes, and not incarnation that creates the *cor inquietum* in Moltmann.[68]

For Alves the basis of hope is the commitment to humanization which is grounded in grace. From the awareness of God comes the need to do what is necessary to make and keep human life in the world human. Hope is deeply related to the power of human creativity, and grace preserves both God's gratuitousness and this human power.

> Messianic humanism, from its historical experience, finds it necessary to preserve both grace and creativity. It therefore rejects the messianism that believes that liberation is created by the powers of man alone and the Protestant destruction of work as the instrument for the creation of history. And as it does this it preserves the critical element of Protestantism and the creative thrust of humanistic messianism. How is this possible? In the context of God's politics of human liberation grace creates the possibility and necessity of man's action. Man is a co-creator. The pact means that God, in the fullness of his eternity, needs, longs, and waits for man. "There is something essential that must come from man" in God's future, Friedmann comments. He "awaits an earthly consummation in and with mankind."[69]

Christian orthopraxis, messianic humanism, liberation—these equivalent expressions—all imply a conjoint project, divine agency and human co-operation, for bringing about the Kingdom. The faith implied by this synergistic project of the Kingdom of God will be our subject in Chapter Three.

Notes

1   See J. Neuner, S.J. and J. Dupuis, S.J., eds., *The Christian Faith in the Historical Documents of the Catholic Church* (Westminster, MD: Christian Classics, 1975), No. 1928/1524, pp. 556–57.

2   Speaking about Liberation Theology as a whole de Gruchy notes that it had located the doctrine of grace firmly in the historical arena of the struggle for justice and liberation. In terms of Catholic liberationists transcending the traditional nature-grace dialectic he writes: "The history of salvation and the history of human liberation and social transformation, while not to be confused, cannot be separated—they belong on the same continuum." (John W. de Gruchy, *Liberating Reformed Theology*, p. 179; see also p. 180).

   On Segundo and Boff de Gruchy writes:

> A close reading of Segundo and Boff will show that they remain Roman Catholic in their understanding of the relationship between nature and grace, and some elements in their thought may cause Reformed theologians to proceed with caution. This is particularly so when the necessary distinction between salvation and liberation is in danger of being confused, thereby leading to unacceptable ecclesial and political consequences. Yet, having transcended the sterility of scholastic debate and rediscovered the biblical perspective on God's gratuitous activity in history and people, their central thrust resonates well with a truly Reformed theology. Both stress the priority of grace, both stress the character of God's grace as God's free gift in Jesus Christ, and both stress that grace liberates people for new relationships that have transforming significance for the world. (de Gruchy, *ibid.*, p. 180)

   It is interesting and strange in the light of what he has written on the liberationists' approach to grace, and the relationship between the Catholic liberationist and Reformed tradition on grace that de Gruchy's book contains not a single reference to Rubem Alves.

3   See for example James A. Lyons, *The Cosmic Christ in Origen and Teilhard de Chardin: A Comparative Study* (New York: Oxford University Press, 1982); see pp. 5, 218.

   Lyons comments that Teilhard believed that his task in Christology was to retrieve a long-neglected New Testament teaching which was essential for accommodating Christianity to the modern world. (Lyons, *ibid.*, p. 5) In carrying out this task, he felt himself to be at one with the Greek Fathers. He was endeavoring to understand Christ in relation to modern science, just as they had attempted to understand Christ within the context of ancient cosmological views.

   According to Lyons, what appeared to be of primary importance to Teilhard was that the evolving world should have a goal. Teilhard did not derive his idea of a goal from evolutionary theory; he took it from Christian eschatology, other Christian sources, Blondel and Scholasticism. Evolution is a category of thought which, in some theological contexts, he uses to provide a more fully elaborated understanding of salvation history. It seems appropriate, then to refer to Teilhard as an evolutionizing Christian. (Lyons, *ibid.*, p. 218) See also Thomas Berry, "The Place of Teilhard in The Christian Tradition," in *Teilhard Perspective* 24:1 (June 1991), pp. 6–7.

In the light of Lyons' comments it is not inappropriate to call Segundo an evolutionizing liberation theologian. Segundo's theology of grace is heavily indebted to Teilhard de Chardin's evolutionist categories. See Frances Stefano, "The Evolutionary Categories of Juan Luis Segundo's Theology of Grace," *Horizons* 19:1 (1992), pp. 7–30; Frances Stefano, *The Absolute Value of Human Action in the Theology of Juan Luis Segundo* (Lanham *et al*: University Press of America, 1992.)

4   See Leonardo Boff, *Liberating Grace* (Maryknoll, N.Y.: Orbis Books, 1979), p. 3. Boff writes:

> Grace is always an encounter between a God who gives himself and a human being who does likewise. By its very nature Grace is the breaking down of realms or worlds that are closed upon themselves. Grace is relationship, exodus, communion, encounter, openness and dialogue. It is the history of two freedoms, the meeting of heaven and earth, of God and humans, of time and eternity. Grace is something more than time, more than history, more than humanity.

5   This concept of "lack of repugnance," indeed, the terminology itself has been abandoned in contemporary theology. See Henri de Lubac, S.J., *The Mystery of the Supernatural*, trans. Rosemary Sheed (New York: Herder & Herder, 1965), pp. 1–24. For a discussion of its place in the history of theology, as well as recent criticisms of the idea, de Lubac writes:

> In these circumstances, still to persist in seeing St. Thomas as the source of our modern dualism, by arguing that 'any concession on the point' must turn St. Thomas into 'an Augustinian', is not a real argument at all, but an admission of defeat (p. 14) . . . Indeed there are many theologians who would go much further, and now declare that they can find no explicit affirmation in St. Thomas of the concrete possibility of a purely natural order—remembering always that this means a complete order, bearing within it its own final end, in the modern sense of the expression. (p. 14.) . . . Some good historians are even more decidedly and radically negative. (p. 16) If we look more closely at the question, it is hardly surprising that the resistance should have been so strong." (p. 17) See also Gutiérrez, *Theology of Liberation*, p. 44.

6   See Henri de Lubac, *The Mystery of the Supernatural*, pp. 23–24. de Lubac writes:

> "Although, as it seems to me, no change need be made in the general economy of past teaching, and although we can still adopt the idea our fathers have left us of our fundamental relationship with our supernatural end, there is still much to be done in accordance both with our actual intellectual requirements and with the present state of theology, and in view of the difficulties which the

development of thought has produced or accentuated there is a need to show more clearly how this key idea remains completely in harmony with the demands of faith."

7   de Lubac, *The Supernatural*, p. 239. de Lubac wrote:

> "But there is more that one can do, as I think I have made clear. Though one cannot reduce everything to the clarity of a simple vision free of all mystery, one can at least advance dialectically to the harmony which lies beyond the apparent opposition. And this will be easier if, taking the notion of God's transcendence with total seriousness, we stop seeing the call to the supernatural and the offer of grace in a chronological series, as though the second is governed by the first: as though God were bound by his own call once uttered, and could not then recall his offer. The offer of grace expresses, in the sphere of moral liberty, the same act of loving kindness that the call to the supernatural expresses in the ontological sphere. Thus there is nothing in the former to diminish beforehand in any way the gratuitousness of the latter. Neither is exterior to the other, and therefore neither comes before the other. There is always the same unique sovereign initiative at work in both, and the only difference lies in relation to us, because we are at once nature and liberty, an ontological tendency and a spiritual will."

8   Gutiérrez, *Theology of Liberation*, p. 44.

9   See Karl Rahner, *Foundations of Christian Faith: An Introduction to the Idea of Christianity*, trans. William V. Dych (New York: Crossroad, 1990); see pp. 126ff. According to Rahner humankind is the event of God's absolute self-communication. This statement refers to absolutely all persons and it expresses an existential of every person. (Rahner, *ibid.*, pp. 126–127).

According to Rahner the standard post-Tridentine and neo-Scholastic theory of nature and grace read as follows:

> Supernatural grace is a reality which we know about from the teaching of the Faith, but which is completely outside our experience and can never make its presence felt in our conscious personal life. We must strive for it, knowing as we do through faith that it exists, take care (through good moral acts and reception of the sacraments) that we possess it, and treasure it as our share in the divine life and pledge and necessary condition for life in heaven.

See Karl Rahner, S. J., *Nature and Grace: Dilemmas in the Modern Church* (New York: Sheed and Ward, 1964), p. 115. Rahner summarizes:

> In short, the relationship between nature and grace is thought of as two layers laid very carefully one on top of the other so that they interpenetrate as little as possible. And accordingly, nature's orientation towards grace is thought of as negatively as possible. Indeed, grace is in fact the most perfect fulfillment of nature; indeed, God the Lord of nature can require man to submit himself to grace, but nature in itself has only a *potentia obedientialis* to do this, thought of negatively as possible; the mere absence of a contradiction in such an elevation of nature. Nature itself can be fulfilled in a purely natural destiny, content

and harmonious in its own sphere, without direct contact with God in the Beatific vision, when it turns in on itself in its immediate self-awareness (as it is in the nature of spirit to do: *reditio completa in seipsum*) it is aware of itself as if it were a "*pure nature.*" To Rahner the standard "*two-tiered*" post-Tridentine view of grace and nature cannot be acquitted of a certain "extrinsicity." (*Ibid.*, p. 118).

Rahner's theology of grace and his idea of the "*Supernatural existential*" were thus geared to revising this "*two-tiered*" theory of nature and grace. According to Rahner God communicates God's Self to humankind in humankind's own reality. That is the mystery and fullness of grace. From this the bridge to the mystery of the Incarnation and the Trinity is easier to find. (*Ibid.*, p. 125) Grace penetrates our conscious life, not only our essence but our existence. (*Ibid.*, p. 129). In this regard we understand Rahner to be saying nothing more than the biblical affirmation that humankind was created in God's image. The purpose of a liberationist anthropology is therefore to work with God in the retrieval of that image. It is the task of humanization.

On this issue see also, Karl Rahner, S.J., *Theological Investigations, Volume 1: God, Christ, Mary and Grace*, trans. Cornelius Ernst, O.P. (Baltimore: Helicon Press, 1961), pp. 297–317.

10   According to de Gruchy the separation of justification and regeneration or sanctification in Luther and Calvin was novel but notional. Otherwise, both of them stand in continuity with Catholic teaching, except in its late medieval corrupted forms. What was central to both Catholic tradition and evangelical doctrine was that we cannot save ourselves through any act of our own merit. Our sinfulness is such that we can only be saved and set free to love and obey God's grace in Jesus Christ alone. No matter how much we may seek to justify ourselves before God, to conform to God's will, it is beyond our capacity to do so. This being so, it is not surprising to discover continuities between Calvin and contemporary Catholic teaching, not on the forensic nature of justification, but on its gratuitous character. (de Gruchy, *ibid.*, p. 158)

See George Yule, "Introduction," in *Luther: Theologian for Catholics and Protestants*, ed. George Yule (Edinburgh: T. & T. Clark, 1985), x. Yule writes that "the centrality of justification by grace was the issue from which Luther never varied." He also writes:

"It is our judgment that Luther's remarkable insights into the nature of God's grace revealed in the coming of Christ is the basis for the unity and renewal of the Church and it is to this we point "

Also Gordon Rupp, "Miles Emeritus? Continuity and Discontinuity between the Young and the Old Luther." in George Yule, ed., *Luther: Theologian for Catholics and Protestants*, *ibid.*, p. 78; Timothy F. Lull, ed., *Martin Luther's Basic Theological Writings* (Minneapolis: Fortress Press, 1989), pp. 502–03; Dietrich Bonhoeffer, *The Cost of Discipleship*, Revised Edition (New York: The Macmillan Co., 1963), p. 52:

"It was not the justification of sin, but the justification of the sinner that drove Luther from the cloister back into the world. The grace he had received was costly grace . . . And it was costly, for, so far from dispensing him from good works, it meant that he must take the call of discipleship more seriously than ever before. It was grace because it cost so much, and it cost so much because it was grace. That was the secret of the gospel of the Reformation—the Justification of the sinner."

11 See Juan Luis Segundo, *Liberation of Theology*, trans. John Drury (Maryknoll, N.Y.: Orbis Books, 1976), pp. 149–50; Rubem A. Alves, *Protestantism and Repression: A Brazilian Case Study*, trans. John Drury, re. Jaime Wright (Maryknoll, N.Y.: Orbis Books, 1985), pp. 12–17. See also Herbert Marcuse, *Reason and Revolution: Hegel and the Rise of Social Theory*, 2d ed. (New York: Humanities Press, 1954), pp. 3, 14, 15, 16.

According to Marcuse the French Revolution not only abolished feudal absolutism, replacing it with the economic and political system of the middle class, but it completed what the German Reformation had begun, emancipating the individual as a self-reliant ruler of his/her life. (Marcuse, *ibid.*, p. 3)

Marcuse argues that ever since the German Reformation, the masses had become used to the fact that, for them, liberty was an 'inner value,' which was compatible with every form of bondage, that due obedience to existing authority was a prerequisite to everlasting salvation, and that toil and poverty were a blessing in the eyes of the Lord. A long process of disciplinary training had introverted the demands for freedom and reason in Germany. One of the decisive functions of Protestantism had been to induce the emancipated individuals to accept the new social system that had arisen, by diverting their claims and demands from the external world into their inner life. Luther established Christian liberty as an internal value to be realized independently of any and all external conditions. "Man learned to turn upon himself his demand for the satisfaction of his potentialities and 'to seek within' himself, not in the outer world, his life's fulfillment." (Marcuse, *ibid.*, p. 14).

12 Elsa Támez, *Amnesty of Grace*, pp. 31, 35–36.

13 Alves, *Protestantism and Repression*, p. 13.

14 Alves, *ibid.*, p. 14. See pp. 15–16, "Protestantism as the Origin of the Monstrous Phenomena of Modern Times."

15 W.A. Visser 't Hooft commented that Calvin was a humanist caring for the restoration of the human person. See W.A. Visser 't Hooft, "Foreword," in André Biéler, *The Social Humanism of Calvin*, trans. Paul T. Fuhrmann (Richmond, Virginia: John Knox Press, 1964), p. 7. Biéler's book is a valuable presentation of Calvin's humanism. Calvin's Christian humanism is grounded in his epistemology and theological methodology for the restoration of humankind. The knowledge of God and ourselves are connected. According to Calvin: "Without knowledge of self there is no knowledge of God. Nearly all the wisdom we possess, that is to say, true and sound wisdom, consists of two parts: the knowledge of God and of ourselves." See *Calvin: Institutes of the Christian Religion, Volume 1*, ed. John T. McNeil, trans. Ford Lewis Battles, Library of Christian Classics, Vol. XX: Book

I.1 To III.xix (Philadelphia: The Westminster Press, 1960), p. 35; also pp. 35–6 n.1.

According to Timothy George when Calvin spoke of the two-fold knowledge of God (*duplex cognitio dei*), he was not talking about the ever-present duality of the divine-human encounter. Rather he referred to the knowledge of God as Creator, manifested in the fashioning of the universe, and the knowledge of God as Redeemer, seen only in the face of Christ. See Timothy George, *Theology of the Reformers* (Nashville, Tennessee: Broadman Press, 1988), p. 189.

There are clear parallels between the humanistic theology of Vatican II which generated Liberation Theology and Calvin's humanism. See, for example, John W. de Gruchy, *Liberating Reformed Theology*, pp. 158, 178. Here again we note de Gruchy's omission of Rubem Alves because Alves is a significant exponent of Calvin's theology in a liberationist key.

16   Calvin, *Selections from His Writings*, ed. John Dillenberger (New York: Anchor Books, Doubleday & Co., Inc., 1971) , p. 268.

17   See Dillenberger, Calvin, *Selections*, pp. 270–71.

18   See Timothy George, *Theology of the Reformers*, pp. 212–22.

19   See Wilhelm Niesel, *The Gospel and the Churches: A Comparison of Catholicism, Orthodoxy and Protestantism*, trans. David Lewis (Philadelphia: The Westminster Press, 1962), p.2.

20   Niesel, *Gospel and the Churches*, p. 191.

21   Niesel, *ibid.*, p. 193.

22   *Ibid.*, p. 194.

23   John de Gruchy comments that for Calvin, human liberation is first and foremost redemption from the bondage of self-worship. All else derives from this act of God's undeserved grace. Through grace we are restored to our true nature as human beings made in the image of God, and therefore reconciled to God and to one another. See de Gruchy, *ibid.*, p. 162.

24   See Rubem A. Alves, *A Theology of Human Hope* (Washington/Cleveland: Corpus Books, 1969), xiii.

25   Rubem Alves, *Theology of Human Hope*, pp. 98–99.

26   See Roger Haight, S.J., *An Alternative Vision: An Interpretation of Liberation Theology* (New York, Mahwah: Paulist Press, 1985), p. 22. According to Haight liberation is taken to include in its meaning social, economic and political release from oppressive structures. God's saving grace is seen to affect not just a person's psychology and spiritual intentions and motivations but the whole of human existence . . . In this thinking of salvation and liberation, the strictly theological datum from the content of faith and the social realities of secular life in history and the world meet in a dramatic way. The uniting of symbol and experience of salvation with historical liberation is a central element in Liberation Theology.

27   See the *Final Document: International Ecumenical Congress of Theology*, February 20–March 2, 1980, São Paulo, Brazil, in *The Challenge of the Basic Christian Communities*. Papers from the International Ecumenical Congress of Theology, February 20–March 2, 1980, São Paulo, Brazil, ed. Sergio Torres and John Eagleson, trans. John Drury (Maryknoll, NY: Orbis Books, 1980), p. 237.

28   *Ibid.*

29   See Frances Stefano, *The Absolute Value of Human Action in the Theology of Juan Luis Segundo*, xxiii n.16. Stefano makes the point that from the beginning action has been central to Segundo's theology. See Juan Luis Segundo, *Función de la iglesia en la realidad rioplatense* (Montevideo: Barreiro y Ramos, 1962), esp. pp. 30–35. Stefano's book is a good study of the place of action in Segundo's theology. On the subject of the totality of action or praxis Stefano writes that action is not synonymous with activity alone but includes the whole spectrum of thinking and willing, knowing and acting, being and doing. It involves negativity, passivity, suffering and endurance as well as positivity, activity and accomplishment. At one and the same time it is doing and an undergoing, a making and a being made, an individual yet sociopolitical affair. Most importantly, it can be adequately understood only in connection with the objective givenness of reality, to which the projective character of action must ultimately conform, by which it is conditioned and facilitated, and in relation to which it has a creative responsibility. Stefano therefore uses the term action as a viable theological synonym for the structure of human existence. (Stefano, *Absolute Value of Human Action*, xix)
      Haight defined praxis as "behavior that is participation in this movement of history; it is a practice or behavior or struggle to increase freedom in history." (Haight, *Alternative Vision*, p. 2, 40–41.).

30   For the evolution of post-Tridentine Catholic theology of grace up to Vatican II see Mertens, "Nature and Grace in Twentieth-Century Catholic Theology," *Louvain Studies* 16 (1991), pp. 242–262.
      On Segundo's theology of grace Stefano makes the point that despite the fact that Segundo begins the series *Theology for Artisans of a New Humanity* with a volume explicitly devoted to the subject of grace, his most constructive contribution to a Jesus-normed theology of co-operative grace occurs in *Jesus of Nazareth Yesterday and Today*. Action is central to this Jesus-normed theology of co-operative grace.
      According to Stefano, after introducing the anthropological foundations of faith and ideologies on which to build, Segundo constructs a liberative interpretation of Jesus' Kingdom and praxis and life-story and then "multiplies" its effectiveness with a theological exegesis of Paul's account in Romans 1–8 of the seemingly inefficacious (but ultimately efficacious) character of human action in an incomplete and tragic universe. Stefano, *Absolute Value of Human Action*, pp. 16–17.

31   On this issue Leonardo Boff comments that for the Protestant Reformers grace was basically the benevolent and merciful attitude of God. It is that attitude that saves sinful humans. There was no systematic reflection on the ontological change in human beings which results from God's attitude. In light of Boff's comment it

is arguable that the Reformers' solution to the problem of grace and human existence had tragic consequences right into the twentieth-century. Boff, however,
noted that the Reformation thinking on grace did elaborate a new horizon for
grace that had a profound impact on the further development of the tract on
grace in both Catholic and Protestant circles. This was the horizon of personal-
ism, with its concomitant categories of dialogue, mutual openness, confidence,
and so forth. In this sense Liberation Theology has gone beyond the mainline
Reformation grace formulations. Liberation Theology is a swing to the "left" or
the Radical Reformation. (See Boff, *Liberating Grace*, p. 11).

32   Segundo, *Liberation of Theology*, trans. John Drury (Maryknoll, NY: Orbis Books,
1976), p. 141.

33   Segundo, *ibid.*, see also "The Pastoral Constitution on the Church in the Modern
World," *Gaudium et Spes* in Austin Flannery, O.P., ed., *Vatican Council II:
Conciliar and Post-Conciliar Documents*, sec. 22. p. 924.

34   See Stefano, *The Absolute Value of Human Action*, xxii n. 13. According to
Stefano this change of focus can be justified by appealing to the universal character of salvation and the gratuitous character of grace. Stefano continues:

> Thanks to grace being everywhere, any and every action done in self-tran-
> scending love, regardless of its connection or lack of connection with religious
> affirmations about Jesus, is action serving the interests of salvation; yet from
> the perspective of the utter gratuitousness of God's love, this is true only
> "negatively" or "indirectly," by reason of the fact that self-transcending love,
> whatever its intramundane source, does not work against the values of God's
> heart: "The one who is not against you is for you" (Mk. 9:40; Lk. 9:50). Non-
> religious persons and groups whose action is self-transcending love are thus
> viewed theologically as living utterly valid lives in their own right, without
> having to be linked to God either explicitly or implicitly by a relation of religious
> faith. In other words, persons and groups who are not disciples and who prac-
> tice self-transcending love are neither opposed to the liberative interests of
> God nor required to. See "The Pastoral Constitution on the Church in the
> Modern World," *Gaudium et Spes*, Flannery, *Vatican II Documents*, Sec. 4,
> p. 904: "At all times the Church carries the responsibility of reading the signs
> of the times and of interpreting them in the light of the Gospel, if it is to carry
> out its task." The Council saw itself as entitled "to speak of a real social and
> cultural transformation whose repercussions are felt on the religious level."
> (*Ibid.*)

35   See "The Pastoral Constitution on the Church in the Modern World," *Gaudium
et Spes, Flannery, Vatican II* Documents, Sec. 4, p. 904: "At all times the
Church carries the responsibility of reading the signs of the times and of interpreting them in the light of the Gospel, if it is to carry out its task." The Council
saw itself as entitled "to speak of a real social and cultural transformation whose
repercussions are felt on the religious level." (*Ibid.*)

36   See "The Pastoral Constitution" *Gaudium et Spes*, Flannery, Sec. 5, p. 907:

The accelerated pace of history is such that one can scarcely keep abreast of it. The destiny of the human race is viewed as a complete whole, no longer as it were, in the particular histories of various peoples: now it merges into a complete whole. And so mankind substitutes a dynamic and more evolutionary concept of nature for a static one, and the result is an immense series of new problems calling for a new endeavor of analysis and synthesis.

37   Segundo, *Theology and the Church*, p. 76.

38   Segundo, *ibid.*

39   *Ibid.*

40   Segundo, *Theology and the Church*, pp. 76–77; see also Section 16, "The Dogmatic Constitution on the Church," *Lumen Gentium*, 21 November, 1964, in Austin Flannery, O.P., Vatican Council II: *The Conciliar and Post- Conciliar Documents* (Collegeville, MN: Liturgical Press, 1975, Fifth Printing, 1980), pp. 367–68.

41   José Míguez-Bonino, *Doing Theology in a Revolutionary Situation*, p. 63.

42   See Alfred T. Hennelly, S.J., "Introduction," in Juan Luis Segundo S.J., *Signs of the Times: Theological Reflections* (Maryknoll, NY: Orbis Books, 1993), p. 2; Juan Luis Segundo, S.J., *Evolution and Guilt*, trans. John Drury (Maryknoll, NY: Orbis Books, 1974), p. 6.

43   Segundo, *Grace and the Human Condition*, p. 176.

44   *Ibid.*

45   *Ibid.*

46   Juan Luis Segundo, "On Absolute Mystery," in *Signs of the Times*, p. 114.

47   Juan Luis Segundo, "The Option for the Poor," in *Signs of the Times*, p. 126.

48   Segundo writes:

God's gift, grace, shows up first as a desire that God has placed within the existence of his people. It was nourished and purified by the preaching of the prophets. Then, with the ushering in of the "now" that echoes through the Pauline letters, it shows up as fulfilled reality. See Segundo, *Theology and the Church*, p. 194.

Alfred Hennelly makes the point that Segundo is indebted to Gustav Lambert for his understanding of the gradual development of revelation in the Bible. See Alfred T. Hennelly, S.J., "Introduction," in *Signs of the Times*, p. 2; Segundo, *Liberation of Dogma*. According to Segundo God's ancient promises are definitively fulfilled in the Bible. They are definitively fulfilled in Jesus Christ. The notion of promise and fulfillment provide the framework to Segundo's *Grace and the Human Condition*. God's grace "prepared" the world for the coming of Jesus Christ. See Segundo, *Grace and the Human Condition*, p. 194.

49   Segundo writes:

> Hermeneutics, stripped of its false limitations and antagonisms, is many things. It is Marxism, criticizing ideologies and looking for social truth that lies buried in structures that alienate man. It is the whole effort undertaken since Freud to unmask the real motives behind human conduct and to restore man to the truth of his projected aims. It is also phenomenology in its deeper sense and its study of inauthentic phenomena.

> Segundo, *Grace and the Human Condition*, p. 33; see also p. 36; Juan Luis Segundo, "Capitalism-Socialism: A Theological Crux," in *Signs of the Times*, pp. 18–23.

50   Segundo comments:

> Thus in his discussion of the ego Freud approaches Marx's problem of alienation, Nietzsche's problem of weakness and we would say, Paul's problem of the inner man who is stripped of control over his efforts by a law that is more powerful than his ego. Thus it is possible to open up a pathway to our theme through Freud's theme of dealing with the ego.

Segundo, Grace and the Human Condition, p. 36.

51   The theme of Medellín was "*The Church in the Present-Day Transformation of Latin America in the Light of the Council.*" See documents, *ibid.* Medellín's reception of Vatican II by reading the signs of the times in Latin America gave official birth to Liberation Theology with its emphasis on *orthopraxis*—theology as lived commitment.

The two major Catholic studies that deal explicitly with grace from a liberationist perspective are: Juan Luis Segundo, *Grace and the Human Condition*, trans. John Drury (Maryknoll, NY: Orbis Books, 1973) and Leonardo Boff, *Liberating Grace*, trans. John Drury (Maryknoll, NY: Orbis Books, 1979).

52   See Stefano, *Absolute Value of Human Action*, ibid., xi. Stefano wrote that in the light of the paralyzing dimensions of evil in our time—what Segundo calls "the whole panorama of human suffering" and what as early as 1917 Walter Rauschenbusch was calling the "bulk of unjust suffering in sight of the modern mind"—the relevance of action and the need to back theological interpretations with a *praxis* of liberation emerge as central concerns. They form the starting-point for virtually all theologies of liberation, among them particularly that of Segundo. He moves from the need for action in the face of such problems toward an interpretation of Jesus' news of God's Kingdom which makes use of a liberative logic internal to action.

Stefano comments that Segundo's familiarity with Blondel's thought does not suggest that his theology is in any way directly influenced by Blondel's philosophy. As Stefano noted on the basis of Segundo's own admission, his theology of grace has been more influenced by Leopoldo Malevez. Segundo studied under Malevez with whom he seemed to share a kindred spirit on the universality of grace and the *initium fidei*.

Stefano claims that Segundo's theology is also conducted in the spirit of a highly creative—almost eclectic and critically interpretative liberative conversation with the philosophy of Nicholas Berdyaev and more recently with the ecological science of Gregory Bateson. In addition, Segundo engages in productive conversation with many others, including Marx and Freud, Darwin and Wallace, Ricoeur and Gadamer, Rahner and Teilhard de Chardin, Bultmann and Niehbuhr, Lukács and Machovec, the Synoptics and John, and above all, Paul. Stefano's list includes the significant partners Segundo dialogues with in the development of his theology. They are mostly European. Latin American and Third World thinkers do not feature in the list, a point noted by Jürgen Moltmann. Stefano's reference to Blondel was to underscore the profound importance in Segundo's anthropology of the priority of the will in human knowledge of God, a priority Blondel shared and which helped to shape the course of Catholic theology in the twentieth-century. (See Stefano, *The Absolute Value of Human Action*, xxviii n. 45.)

Teilhard de Chardin is a dominant influence in Segundo's theology of grace. On this, see for example, Stefano, "The Evolutionary Categories of Juan Luis Segundo's Theology of Grace." *Horizons* 19.1 (1992), pp. 7–30.

53   See "A Conversation with Juan Luis Segundo, S.J.," p. 173.

54   Juan Luis Segundo, *Grace and the Human Condition*, p. 169. See Juan Luis Segundo, *Teologia Abierta I, Iglesia-Gracia* (Madrid, Huesca 30–31 Ediciones Cristianidad S.L., 1983). p. 395.

55   It must be recalled that Marx is one of the sources that Segundo dialogues with in his theology. To a certain extent Segundo, Vatican II and all modern theologies have had to take the Marxist critique of religion seriously. To a large extent liberation theologians seek to respond to the Marxian critique by demonstrating the transformationist nature of the Christian faith. In order to do so they must demonstrate that Christian faith is singularly efficacious in effecting full human liberation. In this regard Theresa Lowe Ching is to the point when she argues that efficacious love is one of the principles that holds Segundo's work together. In arguing that praxis is the principle that generates the ecumenicity of Liberation Theology we claim that all efficacious love is praxis. See Theresa Lowe Ching, R.S.M., *Efficacious Love: Its Meaning and Function in the Theology of Juan Luis Segundo* (Lanham et al: University Press of America, 1989), x.

56   Segundo, *Grace and the Human Condition*, p. 169. Also *Gracia y Condicion Humana* in *Teologia Abierta I: Iglesia-Gracia*, pp. 197–395; see p. 395.

57   Segundo, *Grace and the Human Condition*, p. 169. The Spanish reads: "Que Dios no tiene otro plan sobre nosotros, si no es el asociarnos con su obra creadora frente al universo histérico." *Teologia Abierta I, Iglesia-Gracia*, p. 395. See Segundo, *Liberation of Theology*, pp. 149–151.

Paul, as already noted, is significant to Segundo's theology of grace. This is so especially with respect to the anthropological key to grace in Segundo's theology. Segundo would therefore accept the Lutheran doctrine of the priority of grace but he goes beyond Luther in retrieving the idea of freedom for the construction of a history of liberation and love.

See Haight, *Alternative Vision*, p. 146. Haight comments that in Segundo, especially, the action or effect of grace is essentially a process of humanization.

58 Alves, *Theology of Human Hope*, p. 11. Alves theology is developed in dialogue with a wide range of sources. These include Church and Society in Latin America Iglesia y Sociedade en America Latina, ISAL), The World Council of Churches, WCC, Richard Shaull, Harvey Cox, Dietrich Bonhoeffer, Jürgen Moltmann, Karl Barth, Martin Luther, John Calvin, Teilhard de Chardin, Karl Marx, Herbert Marcuse, Karl Mannheim, Søren Kierkegaard, Albert Schweitzer, Esdra B. Costas. On this see, for example Ruy Otavio Costa, *Toward a Latin American Ethic of Liberation: A Comparative Study of the Writings of Rubem Alves and José Míguez Bonino from the Perspective of the Sources and Substance of Their Social Ethics (Volumes I, II)*, Ph.D. Dissertation: Boston University Press, 1990.

59 Alves understands truth as the power or praxis which liberates humankind. For him theological language must be a liberative language. He writes:

> The shift from abstract truth to truth as praxis represents a movement from Greek ways of thinking to Hebrew ones. The Greek mind combines a deep concern for a-historical truth and theory, as existing in themselves, with contempt for *techne (praxis)*. *Truth is discovered by speculation and pure thought. For the Hebrew mind, on the contrary, truth is derived from praxis. Truth is the name given by a historical community to those acts which were, are, and will be effective for the liberation of man. Truth is act.* For biblical language facts come before words, praxis before theory. Language is a footnote to historical events. (Italics mine).

See Rubem A. Alves, "Theology and the Liberation of Man," in *In Search of A Theology of Development: Papers from a Consultation on Theology and Development* held by SODEPAX in Cartigny, Switzerland, November, 1969, Prepared by Fr. Gerhard Bauer (Geneva: Committee on Society, Development and Peace, 1969), p. 80.

60 Alves, *Theology of Human Hope*, xiii.

61 See Paul Lehmann, *Ethics in a Christian Context* (London: SCM Press, 1963), p. 105. Concerning his indebtedness to Paul Lehmann Alves wrote in *A Theology of Human Hope*, "I am indebted to Prof. Paul Lehmann for the expression "humanistic messianism," which applies perfectly well to our description of political humanism; see *Ideology and Incarnation* (Geneva: John Knox Press, 1962), p. 25, Rubem A. Alves, *A Theology of Human Hope*, p.171 n.27, 44, 55.

62 Alves, *Theology of Human Hope*, pp. 98–99.

63 Jürgen Moltmann, *Theology of Hope: On the Ground and the Implications of a Christian Eschatology* (New York: Harper & Row, 1967). See Douglas J. Schuurman, *Creation, Eschaton, and Ethics: The Ethical Significance of the Creation-Eschaton Relation in the Thought of Emil Brunner and Jürgen Moltmann*, American University Studies, Series VII, Theology and Religion, Vol. 86 (New York *et al*: Peter Lang, 1991), p. 102:

Some interpreters emphasize the discontinuous eschaton and its role. The former often criticize Moltmann for severing eschatology from human history and constructive social transformation. The latter criticize Moltmann for relating eschatology to utopian plans in too direct a manner. Thus Rubem Alves criticizes Moltmann for neglecting continuity and mediation. Langdon Gilkey criticizes Moltmann for positing discontinuity between creation/providence and eschatology, arguing that "if God be merely coming and not here in any sense, then the biblical language of eschatological hope is meaningless."

64   See Harvey Cox, "Foreword," to Alves, *Theology of Human Hope,* xi. On the development of the "Theology of Hope" see M. Douglas Meeks, *Origins of the Theology of Hope* (Philadelphia: Fortress Press, 1974); Richard J. Bauckham, *Moltmann: Messianic Theology in the Making* (Southampton, UK: Marshall Pickering, 1987); Jürgen Moltmann, "Hope," in *The Westminster Dictionary of Christian Theology,* Alan Richardson and John Bowden, eds. (Philadelphia, Pennsylvania: The Westminster Press, 1983), pp. 27–72.

65   See Jürgen Moltmann, "Hope," in Eds. Alan Richardson and John Bowden. *The Westminster Dictionary of Christian Theology.* p. 272.
      According to Moltmann the structure of hope common to the two testaments is sharply different from any extra-biblical expectation: the act of hope is not an extrapolation of the present into an expected future, but it is the anticipation of the promised future itself. The future is already at work in the present in hope for the future of God. (Moltmann, "Hope," p. 271)
      Moltmann claimed that it was Ernst Bloch, going back to biblical and Marxist traditions, who first made the 'Principle of Hope' (his book *Das Prinzip Hoffnung,* 1959) a central subject of philosophical and theological concerns. In the mediation of anthropological hopes and material tendencies through society, Bloch's 'ontology of not-yet-being' aims at overcoming the alienation between humankind and nature. (Moltmann, *ibid.,* p. 271) Bloch therefore helped to take hope out of a restricted view.

66   Moltmann, *ibid.,* p. 272.

67   This is the fundamental critique Alves also levels against the languages of "technologism," existentialism, and Barthianism. They rule out a meaningful place for human action in the mediation of the future. They therefore help to justify the *status quo* and lead to de-humanization. For Alves the question is how can hope be truly transformative and liberative if it is not radically inserted or incarnated in history?

68   Alves, *Theology of Human Hope,* p. 59.

69   Alves, *ibid.,* p. 143.

Chapter 3

Faith and Human Transformation

This chapter seeks to extrapolate further the ecumenicity of Liberation Theology from its understanding of Christian faith as liberative and transformative. As we have seen, Liberation Theology, restores human activity to significance as that activity historically mediates the coming of the Kingdom. The Kingdom is understood as a conjoint divine-human project, the act of God's self-gift for humankind's liberation and humanization. This gift is appropriated through personal commitment and action; it is also longed and waited for in prayer and expectancy. Faith thus operates within a framework both historical and eschatological as a call to total commitment and obedience.

My aim in the chapter is to show more fully how Liberation Theology re-conceptualizes faith, justification, and sanctification within this combined framework of history and eschatology, in this way transcending the traditional religious divisions and polemics surrounding these basic categories. In the first part of the chapter I review the understanding of the relation between faith and justification in post-Reformation Catholic and Protestant theologies. I look then at the traditional conceptualizations of divine and human agency in Christian regeneration. This leads to an articulation of the total process of justification in Liberation Theology understood as liberation. This section is elaborated in two sub-sections: first, the inter-religious consensus on justification as liberation; secondly, integral salvation as full or complete liberation. In the third section I explore Segundo's contribution to this continuing evolution by his reflection on the relation of faith and human transformation, the captivity of faith in Christendom, the dangers of divorcing faith from history, the relation between faith and ideology, and finally the hermeneutical circle. In section four I look at Alves' contribution through his use of the humanistic legacy in the Reformed tradition, with its emphasis on faith as humanly transformative and creative of history.

Faith and Justification in Post-Reformation
Catholic and Protestant Theologies

The liberationist emphasis on praxis as the key to understanding the relation between faith and justification, transcends both the Protestant understanding of faith as "fiducia," and the Catholic emphasis on faith as "assensus." In terms of "assensus" faith is regarded more as belief in or assent to some truth, whether the supernatural truth of the nature of God, or the historical truth of the past. As "fiducia" on the other hand, faith is the basic orientation of the whole person, and while including belief, is best described as trust, confidence, or loyalty.[1] Advocates of faith as "assensus" regard faith as the first step to salvation. It requires for completion the virtues of hope and charity. Advocates of the "fiducia" model see all actions and thoughts of humankind as expressions of a basic orientation, and regard such a basic orientation as constituting the decisive and proper relationship to God.[2] According to Van Harvey, while both Catholics and Protestants agree on the necessity of faith for human regeneration, the basic disagreements between them, as well as among Protestants themselves, may be explained to a great extent in term of these two differing conceptions of faith.[3]

Today the consensus is that the grounds for this post-Reformation divide no longer exist.[4] The possibility of an ecumenical understanding and a new ecumenical theological paradigm is implicitly suggested by this consensus. Liberation Theology in fact represents a theological school or tradition which overcomes this divide in understanding between "fiducia" and "assensus" through its delineation of faith as praxis. Faith is here a holistic praxis, a total orientation of one's being, the ground where all human alienations are overcome.[5] Justification, the reception of God's gratuitous, reconciling, and forgiving grace, is thus seen not purely as a private reality but in terms of complete transformation in history.

The liberationist shift in understanding rests on the foundation that the concerns and interpretive stresses which were of primary importance for the sixteenth century Reformation no longer apply in contemporary experience. There is a common inter-religious concern and hermeneutic of Latin American oppression and conditions of dehumanization. Liberation theologians have a common understanding of the meaning and significance of each other's doctrines in the light of these conditions. Out of this commonality is generated a passionate convergence whose aim is an informed Christian theological commitment to bringing an end to this experience and history of oppression.

Our representative theologians, Segundo and Alves, from their different perspectives, share this concern, consensus, and ultimate aim. Faith for both is the freedom in which human beings and God work together in the praxis of liberation and humanization of Latin American peoples. Faith's commitment leads to the doing of justice through which the oppressed are restored to fuller life. Justification is not simply the condition of the individual soul at right with God; it includes a redemption of the whole created and historical order according to the norm of the Kingdom of God. This understanding of justification means correlative changes in the understanding of sanctification.

Sanctification shifts from the private realm of inner holiness and perfection to include the public, historical realm of realizing the presence of the Kingdom in history. It therefore involves politics, the task of converting the kingdoms of this world into the Kingdom of God and of Christ.

Faith and Sanctification: Traditional Understandings of Divine and Human Agency in Christian Regeneration

Traditional Catholic understandings of the relation between faith and sanctification have been set within an individual-ontological/psychological framework.[6] The turn to a dialectic of grace and history, as we saw, reformulates this within a communal, historical, and eschatological framework, in which divine and human causalities operate together in human transformation. This implies a shift from a theology in which sanctification has no real historical significance to one in which it has. As one of the benefits of Jesus Christ, sanctification has significance in terms of history being made holy. Earthly values and actions are eschatologically valuable in terms of the building of the Kingdom in history.

Traditionally, sanctification, which derives from the Latin "sanctus," meaning "holy," described the process in which new life (regeneration) was imparted to the believer by the Holy Spirit, with the effect that he/she was released from the compulsive power of sin and guilt and enabled to love God and serve his/her neighbor.[7] Sanctification meant personal liberation. In Roman Catholicism there was no significant division between justification and sanctification. Sanctifying grace was required to remit original sin and to impart to the soul a new and higher disposition or virtue that would make possible the salutary acts leading to final salvation, that is, the beatific vision. The entire life of the believer was to be growth from "grace to grace," faith leading to hope and charity.

Growth in grace was closely linked to the sacramental and penitential system of the Church, for the remission and forgiveness of post-baptismal sins was essential for the final salvation or justification of the believer. Since it was believed that a special infusion of grace was necessary for the eradication of all sin, and since no one was assured that he/she would not fall from grace, final forgiveness and justification were identical with complete sanctification.[8]

The Reformers, on the other hand, tended to make a sharp distinction between justification and sanctification. Luther shifted his doctrine from the Augustinian model of a progressive imputation of grace.[9] He separated justification from sanctification, relegating the latter to eschatological status. Between justification and sanctification there was the praxis of active love. For Luther the believer who was gratuitously justified and set at liberty from pre-occupation with guilt and personal salvation was also set at liberty to fulfill God's law.

Calvin assumed the Lutheran understanding of justification but went beyond Luther to make sanctification the central principle of the Christian faith. The re-humanization of humankind in Jesus Christ was central to Calvin's perspective. If Luther stressed that justification set the Christian at liberty, Calvin emphasized that the Christian was set at liberty to recover his/her lost humanity through Jesus Christ. A praxis of humanization was thus central to Calvin's doctrine of sanctification.

Liberation Theology has gone beyond Calvin's thought by setting the praxis of sanctification within a historical-eschatological framework. For Bonino, sanctification is not to be measured by an ideal norm of perfection, or (as against Wesley) an equally unreal purity of motivation. The criterion is the concrete demand of the present Kairos. Some action, or project, or achievement is required of us in the present, which embodies the service of love, and reflects a mature form of obedience.[10]

Sanctification for Bonino is thus the praxis of doing God's will as that will is manifest in and through historical Latin American exigencies: It means that the Church is given a specific task, which enshrines the meaning and purpose of the covenant. Believers are active partners in this mission and are sanctified through it.[11]

Justification as Liberation

The traditional distinction (or demarcation) between liberation and sanctification should not obscure the fact that in Liberation Theology the category of liberation describes justification's total process, inclusive of sanctification. What is underlined is a transformed human community of persons, beyond the deformations of oppressive experience and history. The total process is the object of common theological clarification and emphasis. As Boff expressed it, a grace which is social and liberative criticizes and unmasks those in power, and underlines the continent's yearning for complete development.[12]

Grace is thus clearly another name for liberation.[13] Similarly, for Elsa Támez justification means liberation, or "the solidarity of God," and "the affirmation of life."[14] The God who justifies is the God who condemns everything that threatens the life of God's people, everything that enslaves them. The glory of God the Father/Mother is seeing God's sons and daughters come to maturity by faith, a capacity granted by the gift of justification.[15]

For Boff and Támez, justification re-read and re-interpreted as total liberation, with social, historical, and eschatological dimensions, represents a Christian theological necessity. Individualism, subjectivism, and passivity have contributed to a distortion and confusion of its essential meaning. The reformulated liberation agenda is not a form of contemporary polemics. The concern is rather existential, that is, seen and felt from the point of view of the experience of suffering people. From this perspective the issue, as Araya put it, is not "how can I experience a merciful God, (Lutheran)?" or "How can I become free of guilt and sin (Catholic)?," but "How can we bring about a just world?," or "How can we be merciful?"[16]

Total Liberation as Liberation from Sin

Liberation Theology does not attenuate or strip significance from the close relation between justification and sin. Sin, the opposite of liberation, represents whatever is radically opposed to the Kingdom of God. As The Final Document of the International Ecumenical Congress of Theology put it:

> The liberation and life offered by God surpass everything that we can achieve in history. But these are not offered outside history nor by bypassing history[17]

Like liberation itself, sin is viewed in historical-eschatological terms. It is also contextualized and freed from individual, abstract and generic connotations. With these connotations and in a context where the sins that kill are very tangible, justification means good news for the oppressor, not for the poor. The oppressor can feel pardon for sin and relief from guilt without confronting the wrath of God or the judgment of God, and without the need for conversion or any change of practice.[18]

Conversion, the fruit of justification, or from another perspective the commitment to liberation, implies a social praxis which generates freedom and life for persons, and an end to oppression. While sin cannot be reduced to social injustice, it is vital to see, liberationists insist, that any dehumanizing situation is an offense against God, and for that reason a manifestation of sin. A spiritualization of sin has made it difficult to make identifications in concrete realities—a precondition necessary for struggling against sin itself. The transformation issuing from the forgiveness of sin should mean the efflorescence of the justice of God, not concealment and maintenance of sin in new guises and under new names.

Faith and Transformation in Segundo

Segundo and Alves both accept the emphases so far explored in Liberation Theology: liberation as the total process of justification, a conjoint project of divine-human agency, a conversion from sin and commitment to making manifest the justice of God. Both theologians, however, also explore further presuppositions and dimensions of a transformative faith, in such a way that taken together the liberation ecumenical consensus on justifying faith becomes more comprehensively amplified.

The exercise of a transformative faith for Segundo implies first a critique of faith as held captive by the culture of Christendom. Christendom manifested one of the basic temptations that threaten faith, namely a divorce from history and the commitments of life.[19] Segundo's concern is to bring the two poles or realms back into relation and dialogue.

In *The Liberation of Dogma,* Segundo argues that Christendom was coterminous with the medieval period, in which ecclesiastical structure linked to feudalism became increasingly built up, centralized, and sacralized.[20] The medieval Church found itself set in a privileged situation.[21] Philosophically and theologically also, the attempted synthesis of Augustine was perfected by the genius of Aquinas with the help of Aristotelian categories. A number of implications arose as a result of this synthesis.

First, Aquinas' vision of existence and the world served as a perfect framework and vehicle for revelation. Philosophy was the handmaid, the servant, of theology.[22] Aquinas' synthesis, secondly, achieved the perfect unity of knowledge, neatly arranged in hierarchical form. In humankind the soul was higher than and ruled the body, the passions were subject to the will, and the will to the intellect; the intellect was subordinate to faith. Nature was the epiphany of God; its different realms were hierarchically arranged to serve humankind and to facilitate dialogue with God. Human relationships formed concentric circles, moving out from the family, to social classes, to political society. Ultimately, through the Church, these relationships were all subordinated to God. Humankind saw the historical process as so many preparatory steps to salvation; one age succeeded another, moving towards the encounter with Christ. The present was the final age before the parousia. The human adventure itself was a journey out of the dark shadows cast by the fall into the light of Christ, where all partial truths found their full expression, were a prelude to religious realities, and such realities a preparation for the Christian religion.

In this comprehensive medieval synthesis the world lost its autonomy through integration into the religious view. This religious view was definitive, because once the structures and institutions were seen as part of the divine order, they became rigid and static.[23] Segundo summarizes his characterization of Christendom's basic flaw as a strong temptation to immobilism, arising from the synthesis of knowledge and the hierarchical structuring of reality. All curiosity or search is regarded with horror. Inquiry tended to be anesthetized by the fear that it would break this magic spell of peace and order in society, knowledge and religious practice.[24]

Under its immobilist synthesis Christendom held faith and faith's historical dimensions captive. A dualism also crept into the understanding of faith, which held that the world had no significance in terms of salvation. The divorce of faith from history and the world led the Church to being "traitorous," because its essence and function is to be in dialogue with the world. In Segundo's view, the Church tied faith to a specific and static image of the world,[25] and increased the chasm between both.[26] It grew distrustful of the sense and thrust of history,[27] and this prevented her from seeing that this sense and thrust was a permanent feature of salvation history. She was also prevented from dialoguing with the world, whose thought became more and more bound up with historical becoming. All this spelled calamity for the Church, because her essence and function are defined in terms of dialogue and service to the world.[28]

In the light of this history, according to Segundo, the most urgent task for releasing faith from captivity, is evangelization: letting faith reach people as "good news."[29] To reach people as good news, the essentials of faith must be recovered. This implies going back twenty centuries, since from then on the essentials have become gradually coated by things that were true and respectable but accidental, secondary additions.[30] The task of evangelization for Segundo begins not by talking but listening to the expectations of humankind. This is something the Church does not do; she thinks she already knows what evangelization is, independent of the expectations of humankind. What is worse is that the Church distrusts this listening, which is considered horizontalizing the faith, and dangerous because merely human answers are given, not answers in faith. The Church prefers to give answers without regard to expectations. Thus the good news aspect of evangelization completely disappears.[31]

With evangelization goes action. Faith, for Segundo, if it is to be "good news," must not be just a matter of intellectual assent, which turns it into a possession of the Church, but the total human commitment that risks itself in the building up of the Kingdom in response to the cries and agonies of humankind for authentic humanization. Faith as intellectual assent divorced from the specifics of history ends by endorsing the prevailing status quo instead of being truly redemptive in the cause of greater humanization. But does faith in relation to and serving the Kingdom not become an ideology of the Kingdom?

Faith and Ideology

For Segundo, faith and ideology are inextricably linked.[32] Faith is not an ideology, but it has sense and meaning only as it serves as the foundation for ideologies.[33] According to Segundo we recognize an ideology in the fact that it has no pretensions about representing any objectively absolute value.[34] An ideology is only worth as much as the arguments that support it. This feature distinguishes the founders of ideologies from the founders of religions. The former try to convince people with arguments, the latter appeal to the fact that they possess some absolute value.

Faith relativizes any and every particular ideology, though it does not relativize the general need for ideologies in orienting one's life.[35]

As Segundo put it: "Having faith makes no sense if it does not lead me to give direction to my life. At the same time, however, the direction that faith gives my life is relativized by the faith itself."[36]

Thus, Christians cannot avoid the necessity of inserting something to fill the void between their faith and their options in history. The turn to and use of ideologies is inevitable.[37] So understood, the relation between faith and ideology still requires further clarification. The difficulty, as Alves saw it, was our habit of envisaging faith as occupying a plane of eternal certitudes, to be professed on the one hand, and to be translated into action on the other. Yet, we may have to understand faith in the opposite sense, as a radically historical mode of being, as openness to what is provisional and relative.[38]

Segundo also calls into question a faith understanding which is fundamentally dualistic. This ethos is based on the separation between the natural and the supernatural which, as Chapter Two showed, was officially abandoned by Vatican II, a situation that provided a springboard for the development of Liberation Theology. The liberation ethos is based not on this dualism and separation, but on the dialectical interpenetration of transcendence and history. Faith is thus for Segundo a process whereby humankind submits, a process of learning in and through ideologies how to handle new and unforeseen situations in history.[39] It makes no Christian sense to put distance between ideologies and faith in order to preserve and safeguard faith: "Without ideologies faith is as dead as a doornail, and for the same reason that James offers in his epistle: it is totally impracticable (Jas 2:17)."[40] Faith is finally not a universal, atemporal, pithy body of content which sums up divine revelation once the latter has been divested of ideologies. On the contrary, it is maturity by way of ideologies, the possibility of fully and conscientiously carrying out the ideological task on which the real-life liberation of human beings depend.

The Hermeneutic Circle

Another crucial dimension of a transforming faith in Segundo's theology is the task of interpreting the Word of God as it is addressed to us here and now.[41] An approach which attempts to relate past and present, Segundo argues, in dealing with the Word of God has to have its own special methodology—the hermeneutic circle.[42]

For Segundo the hermeneutical circle is the continuing change in Christian interpretation of the Bible, dictated by the continuing change in present-day individual and social reality. The circular nature of this interpretation stems from the fact that each new reality requires a fresh interpretation of the Word of God, which changes reality accordingly, making in turn for re-interpretation of the Word, thence again to reality, back to the Word, and so on.[43] His understanding, Segundo claims, deserves its designation more than Bultmann's.[44] His argument is that there are two preconditions which must be accepted in the hermeneutic circle, otherwise theology will always be a conservative way of thinking and acting.[45]

The first precondition is that the questions rising out of the present be rich, general, and basic enough to force persons to change their customary conceptions of life, death, knowledge, society, politics, and the world in general. Only a change of this sort, or at least a pervasive suspicion about personal ideas and value judgments concerning those realities will enable persons to reach the theological level and force theology to return to reality and ask itself new and decisive questions.[46]

The second precondition is that if theology assumes it can respond to the new question without changing its customary interpretation of the Scriptures, this stance immediately terminates the circle. Moreover, if our interpretation of Scripture does not change along with the problems, the problems themselves will go unanswered, or worse, they will receive old, conservative, unserviceable answers.[47]

Both these preconditions show how Segundo is concerned to maintain the integrity of Liberation Theology as critical reflection on reality in the light of the Word. As he put it: "Liberation deals not so much with content as with the method used to theologize in the face of our real-life situation."[48] In this process Scripture is experienced as the living and liberating Word in history, its truth as good news, God's power for liberation. Segundo's hermeneutic circle in fact summarizes his theological method in its quadrilateral process.

1. The way of experiencing reality which leads to ideological suspicion;
2. The application of ideological suspicion to the prevailing superstructure in general and to theology in particular;
3. The new way of experiencing theological reality that leads to exegetical suspicion, that is, to the suspicion that the prevailing interpretation of the Bible has not taken important pieces of data into account;
4. The new hermeneutics, that is, the new way of interpreting the fountain head of the faith (Scripture) with the new elements at our disposal.[49]

Segundo's proposal/understanding of the hermeneutical circle points to the emergence of an authentic Latin American "logos."[50] It seeks to bring the transformative dimensions of Christian faith into radical engagement with the human tragedy in Latin America, with the vital flesh and blood questions of the struggling peoples of the continent. Of this agenda Segundo writes:

If we understand and appreciate the hermeneutic circle, then we will also understand and appreciate something that is very important for Latin American theology of liberation. When it is accused of partiality, it can calmly reply that it is partial because it is faithful to Christian tradition rather than to Greek thought. It can also say that those who attack it are even more partisan, though they may not realize it, and tend to muzzle the Word of God by trying to make one particular portion of Scripture the Word of God not only for certain particular moments and situations, but for all situations and all moments.[51]

Segundo's proposal is radically historical and evangelical. Christian faith—unlike a system captive to Greek thought—is transformative in human and historical terms. It invites persons to participate with God in the historical mediations of the Kingdom to which it points, and from which it draws its energy and drive. Faith thus involves commitment and praxis, which leads to the creation of history afresh as history and experience mediate the pressing demands of the Word.

Alves: Faith as the Transformation of Experience and the Creation of History

Alves' understanding of faith's transformative character stems from the inherited emphasis and concern in Reformed theology for human restoration. This legacy is rooted in Calvin's theology of grace and sanctification. Calvin's anthropocentric/theocentric perspective ("There is no question of God which is not simultaneously a question of humankind, and no question of humankind which is not simultaneously a question about God.") was set within a covenantal/communal, or 'koinonia' framework.[52] Alves' theology is indebted to this originating perspective as to its more contemporary forms and redescriptions in the theologies of Moltmann and Lehmann.

In *The Theology of Human Hope*, Alves uses Lehmann's normative question, "What does it take to make and to keep human life in the world human?," is to address critically Moltmann's reflection on hope. He concludes that Moltmann remains insufficiently dialectical. Moltmann is unable to offer any authentic paradigm for historical liberation or guidance to Christians struggling to discover how to speak faithfully the language of faith in the context of their concrete, historical commitment to humanization. At the end, Alves feels Moltmann comes close to Bultmann and Barth: what makes human life human in the world, namely, transcendence, is mediated by an act of consciousness as it looks back to a certain event of the past. Only the word of promise points to God's presence in the world, to God's elusiveness, God's future.[53]

Alves' concern to bring Christian faith into closer relation with the historical struggle for liberation caused him to go beyond the Reformed humanistic tradition, making it more radically historical and dialectical in its understanding of faith. The result is that he retrieves human activity in terms of its mediation of human liberation.

The language of faith is for Alves the expression of liberation. It is derived from the concrete commitment of many Christians to the task of freeing persons from the powers that keep them in bondage. In this process Christians are confronted by the language of political humanism, which radically criticizes any language that speaks of "*theos.*"[54] The encounter provides the occasion or '*kairos,*' for the death and resurrection of both the language of faith and that of political humanism.[55] The result, as Segundo noted in the relation of faith to ideology, is a faith-language of a special sort, not eternal and a-historical, but radically historical, and at home with tentativeness and provisionality.[56]

Like Segundo, Alves' understanding of faith is faith as potentially captive and needing to be ceaselessly liberated to be in keeping with its proper nature and for promoting the vision and deed of human liberation. While the basic import of Segundo's thought is in the hermeneutic circle, Alves expresses it in terms of the iconoclastic and subversive potentiality of faith-language. This language is one of negative vigilance in the face of any absolute. It keeps its secondary character, its quality of footnote, its permanent reference to the praxis, which mediates to history a new possibility of human life.[57]

In other words the substance and function of Christian faith is liberation and humanization. Faith is not knowledge of something.[58] Against those who would argue that Christian faith is reactionary, a virtual "opiate of the masses," Alves is an apologist on its behalf. To Alves, Christian faith is historically relevant in that it offers an authentic paradigm for humanization which, as we saw in Chapter Two, he defined as messianic humanism. Christian faith is an imperative with historical application in terms of creating an alternative history of humanization.[59] Where history offers nothing but objective uncertainties, in faith consciousness discovers an infinite passion. Faith is something sheerly gratuitous, something existing in spite of. It has no special content; it is simply itself; absolute and undirected. In Tillich's words, it is ultimate concern.[60]

Faith is also radically subversive of absolutism because its horizon is eschatological. Faith thus forbids the crystallization of an absolute language.[61] Since the experience of faith cannot be expressed directly, all forms of language are inadequate. In Alves' own words, "faith rules out dogma."[62] It is not intellectual assent to a revealed proposition nor a rule of practice in which behavior is subjected to a series of formulas which differentiate between what is commanded and what is prohibited.[63] Alves' argument is that such an understanding of faith leads to the elimination of mediations and the separation of faith from history;[64] Segundo's major theological concern is thus a key point of convergence between the two theologians. The assertion of faith is not "I know that" but rather "I wager that."[65] When pondered radically, the faith experience prohibits its infinite passion from being crystallized verbally as an object of knowledge.[66] The language of faith is a language of symbols, not a language of signs.[67] Signs point directly and univocally to the objects to which they refer; the communication is direct. Symbols never communicate directly because what is to be communicated by them transcends rationality which is normative within the limits of experience.[68] The language of faith is not absolutist and interpretative but transformative, liberative and gratuitous. Truth is appropriated at the risk of uncertainty, it is a magical temptation to eliminate doubt. The human mode of existence ceases to be gratuitous when a segment of the finite is absolutized.[69]

Faith leads to the transformation of experience and the creation of history; it is the midwife of the future. Faith is at the service of mediating the perfect which is to come symbolized by the Kingdom of God.[70] Thus understood faith is not opposed to doubt which necessarily questions all attempts at absolutization.[71] Theological language, as the language of faith, is the truth which makes humankind free:

> What is faith if not readiness to risk, without certainties in the pocket, in a total openness to the future, in the hope that the future will bring the verification—or fulfillment—of the promises? This is the "spirit" which moves the language of faith, and which determines a life which is a permanent "experiment," always open, life which lives not by its truths but by faith, hope, and love?"[72]

Christian faith involves an imperative which is praxis. According to Alves, it articulates an ongoing activity which mediates a new future to humankind.[73] It retrieves human activity within the specific dispensation of the eschatological horizon of the Kingdom of God. In keeping with the Reformed-Calvinistic tradition out of which he writes Alves clearly understands Christian faith to be against all forms of idolatry.[74] Idolatry subverts human freedom by divinizing or absolutizing temporal realities which arrest humankind's transformation. It inhibits humankind's progress toward its true end and authentic humanization symbolized in the Kingdom of God. In other words while idolatry is enslaving, faith is liberating and humanizing. Humankind must be liberated from idolatry if it is to attain its ultimate goal of being restored to its proper place in the eschatological community of God and all humankind. This is but another way of saying that Christian faith is ecumenical. It provides the authentic paradigm of human liberation and self-realization, pointing to the ultimate transformation of experience and history.

Alves' understanding of faith is thus at several points similar to Segundo's. Faith is God's gracious invitation to humankind to participate in the historical mediations of the Kingdom to which it points, and from which it draws its energy. Faith involves commitment and praxis, which leads to the re-creation of history and the restoration of humankind in light of the exigencies of the Word of God. This understanding of faith creates an ecumenical understanding of the Church, and the foundation for ecumenical activity. According to Alves:

> The structural analysis of . . . the consciousness of the community of faith . . .
> opens new avenues for our understanding of ecclesiology and of the basis for
> ecumenical activity.[75]

The faith-praxis of participation with God in the historical mediations of the Kingdom of God thus provides the basis for an ecumenical ecclesiology and praxis. This latter dimension of Liberation Theology will be developed in the following chapter.

Notes

1 See article on "Faith." by Van A. Harvey in Van A. Harvey, *A Handbook of Theological Terms* (New York/London: Collier Books, Macmillan Publishing Company, Collier Macmillan Publishers, 1964), p. 95.

2 *Ibid.*

3 *Ibid.*

4 See Karl Lehmann and Wolfhart Pannenberg, eds., *The Condemnations of the Reformation Era: Do They Still Divide?* trans. Margaret Köhl (Minneapolis: Fortress Press, 1990), p. 68. The conclusion was:

> Fundamentally, we may undoubtedly, and without any reservation, sum up as follows. Where the interpretation of the justification of the sinner is concerned, the mutual sixteenth-century condemnations which we have discussed no longer apply to our partner today in any sense that could divide the churches . . . We no longer fight against bogus adversaries, and we are careful to express ourselves in such a way that our partner does not even misunderstand us— indeed, can respect our particular 'concern,' even if he is not himself able to adapt our way of thinking and speaking.

See also George A. Lindbeck, "The Framework of Catholic-Protestant Disagreement," in Ed. T. Patrick Burke, *The Word in History: The St. Xavier Symposium* (New York: Sheed and Ward, 1966), pp. 112–19. Lindbeck writes:

> My own personal conclusion to these reflections is that, in the contemporary eschatological-historical framework of thought, it is becoming increasingly difficult to develop a comprehensive and consistent theological justification for either Protestantism or Roman Catholicism as they now exist.

See Hans Küng, *Justification: The Doctrine of Karl Barth and a Catholic Reflection* (Philadelphia: The Westminster Press, 1981), p. 284.

Finally, see The Report of the Joint Lutheran/Roman Catholic Study Commission on "The Gospel and the Church." in *Lutheran World* XIX:1 (1972), pp. 259–273, esp. pp. 263, 264.

5 According to Frances Stefano action is not synonymous with activity alone but includes the whole spectrum of thinking and willing, knowing and acting, being and doing. It involves negativity, passivity, suffering and endurance, as well as positivity, activity and accomplishment. It is simultaneously a doing and an undergoing, a making and a being made, an individual yet sociopolitical affair. See Frances Stefano, *The Absolute Value of Human Action in the Theology of Juan Luis Segundo*, xix.

6 See Leonardo Boff, *Liberating Grace*, p. 151. Boff's work is very important on the issue of traditional and liberationist understanding of justification and faith. The following points made by Boff are noted:

1. Tradition elaborated the lengthy track on justification from *a totally individualistic standpoint*.

2. Moreover, due to the theoretical tools of late scholastic theology and ontology that it employed, Trent did not consider justification as an evolving process akin to the ongoing process of conversion. It did not see it as a slow but steady rejection of a project turned away from God and acceptance of a new project centered more and more on God and Jesus Christ. It viewed justification in fairly watertight compartments, each phase had its own self-contained meaning, e.g., the preparation for justification, justification itself, and the effects of justification. Thus the Christian experience was elaborated in *ontological terms*. This is legitimate enough. But if the Christian experience is not considered in historical terms, in terms of a process, then it tends to remain in abstract formulas wholly apart from living experience. The idiom used seems to have no connection with a concrete praxis of conversion and the living out of the Christian project.

3. Instead of using the term "justification" (a key word in the theology of Paul and the Council), I shall use the term "liberation." It is the same reality, but now elaborated in terms of its dynamic, historical dimensions.

7   See "Sanctification," in Van A. Harvey, *A Handbook of Theological Terms*, pp. 214–15.

8   See Van Harvey, "Sanctification."

9   See George, Theology of the Reformers, p. 74.

10   See José Míguez-Bonino, "Wesley's Doctrine of Sanctification From a Liberationist Perspective," in *Sanctification and Liberation: Liberation Theology in the Light of the Wesleyan Tradition*, ed., Theodore Runyon (Nashville, Tennessee: Abingdon, 1981), p. 63.

Bonino also writes: If faith is to be believed in the realm of history, as history, we cannot imagine a transcendental self that would relate to God apart from a historical self that acts in history. (Bonino, *ibid.*, p. 50).

11   Bonino, *ibid*.

12   Boff, *Grace*, p. 29.

13   Boff, *ibid.*, pp. 22, 35, 151–52.

14   Elsa Támez, *The Amnesty of Grace: Justification by Faith from a Latin American Perspective*, trans. Sharon H. Ringe (Nashville: Abingdon Press, 1993), pp. 14, 155, 166.

15   Támez, *Amnesty of Grace*, p. 145.

16   Támez, *ibid.*, p. 27.

17   See "The Final Document," in *The Challenges of the Basic Christian Communities*. Papers from the International Ecumenical Congress of Theology, February 20-March 2, 1980, São Paulo, Brazil, p. 237.6.

18   Támez, *Amnesty of Grace*, p. 21.

19 See "A Conversation with Juan Luis Segundo, S.J.," in *Faith: Conversations with Contemporary Theologians*, Ed. Teófilo Cabestrero, trans. Donald A. Walsh (Maryknoll, N.Y.: Orbis Books, 1980), p. 173. This conversation is one of the places in which Segundo expressed his views on the subject of the relationship between faith and history and the need for the liberation of faith from traditional orthodoxy in order that the evangelical dimensions of faith may be released for personal and historical transformation.

20 See Segundo, *Liberation of Dogma*, pp. 136–37.

21 Segundo, *The Community Called Church*, p. 116.

22 *Ibid.*

23 *Ibid.*

24 Segundo, *The Community Called Church*, p. 116.

25 Segundo, *ibid.*, p. 117.

26 *Ibid.*

27 *Ibid.*

28 See Segundo, *ibid.*, p. 117.

29 See "A Conversation with Juan Luis Segundo, S.J." in Cabestrero, p. 174.

30 Segundo, *ibid.*, p. 175.

31 *Ibid.*

32 See Segundo, *The Liberation of Theology*, pp. 102, *et al.*

33 *Ibid.*, p. 109.

34 *Ibid.*, pp. 106–7.

35 *Ibid.*

36 *Ibid.* Italics mine.

37 Segundo, *The Liberation of Theology*, p. 109. See Gerhard Ebeling, *The Nature of Faith*, trans. Ronald Gregor Smith (Philadelphia: Fortress Press, 1967).

38 Segundo, *The Liberation of Theology*, pp. 109–110.

39 Segundo, *The Liberation of Theology*, p. 120.

40 *Ibid.*, p. 121; see also p. 181.

41 Segundo, *ibid.*, p. 8.

42 Segundo, *ibid.* Segundo's definition of the hermeneutical circle is one of his distinctive contributions to Liberation Theology. His emphasis is not so much on content but on method. Praxis and commitment are at stake here. Segundo

acknowledged his indebtedness to Bultmann's definition of the hermeneutical circle. Alistair Kee argues that the analysis in Segundo's hermeneutical circle derives from Marx but departs from Marx without any justification. See Alistair Kee, *Marx and the Failure of Liberation Theology* (London: SCM Press; Philadelphia: Trinity Press International, 1990), pp. 184, 182–89, 283. Kee's critique is that liberation theologians have not taken Marx's critique of religion seriously enough. The issue for liberation theologians, as for Marx, was not simply the matter of interpreting history but transforming history; see Karl Marx, *Theses on Feuerbach* in Karl Marx, Frederick Engels, *Collected Works, Volume 5: Marx and Engels: 1845–47* (New York: International Publishers, 1975), pp. 3–5, 6–9, espec. xv, pp. 5, 8, 9, Thesis 11: The philosophers have only *interpreted* the world in various ways; the point, however, is to *change* it. The question in Segundo's case is whether he is explicitly critical of Bultmann's existentialist approach in his hermeneutical circle. Segundo must be necessarily critical of Bultmann because of his unified theory of grace and history. In this sense Segundo is also a heir of Malevez; see L. Malevez, S.J., *Le Message Chrétien et Le Mythe: La Théologie de Rudolf Bultmann* (Bruxelles et al: Desclée de Brouwer, 1954). Rubem Alves has also critiqued Bultmann's existentialism, it does not offer an authentic paradigm of humanization for Latin America because it is fundamentally individualistic and a-historical (Alves, *Theology of Human Hope*, ibid.). Bultmann's existentialism offers no historical mediations which can effectively overcome dehumanization in Latin America. On this issue see also Anselm K. Min versus Schubert Ogden in "How Not To Do a Theology of Liberation: A Critique of Schubert Ogden," *Journal of the American Academy of Religion* 57.1 (Spring, 1989).

43　Segundo, *The Liberation of Theology.*

44　*Ibid.*

45　Segundo, *The Liberation of Theology*, p. 9.

46　Segundo, *ibid.*, pp. 8–9.

47　Segundo, *ibid.*, p. 9.

48　*Ibid.*

49　Segundo, *The Liberation of Theology.*

50　On this issue see Horace Cerutti-Guldberg, "Actual Situation and Perspectives of Latin American Philosophy for Liberation," *The Philosophical Forum* 20:1–2 (Fall-Winter, 1988–89), pp. 43, p. 59 n.2.

51　Segundo, *Liberation of Theology*, pp. 33–34.

52　See Calvin: *Inst.* 1.1.1. McNeil and Battles, p. 35.

53　Alves, *A Theology of Human Hope*, pp. 65–66.

54　Alves, *A Theology of Human Hope*, p. 159; see also xiii.

55　*Ibid.*

56 Alves, *ibid.*, p. 71. See Ebeling, *The Nature of Faith.*

57 Alves, *A Theology of Human Hope,* p. 165.

58 Rubem A. Alves, *Protestantism and Repression,* p. 51.

59 Alves, *Protestantism and Repression,* p. 51.

60 *Ibid.*

61 Alves, *ibid.*, p. 53.

62 *Ibid.*

63 Alves, *ibid.*, p. 59.

64 *Ibid.*

65 Alves, *Protestantism and Repression,* p. 51.

66 Alves, *ibid.*, pp. 51, 53.

67 Alves, *ibid.*, p. 52. Also Rubem Alves, "From Paradise to the Desert: Autobiographical Musings," in *Frontiers of Theology in Latin America,* ed. Rosino Gibellini, trans., John Drury (Maryknoll, N. Y.: Orbis Books, 1979), p. 298. Alves writes: "It is precisely for that reason that religion makes use of symbols rather than signs. The function of a symbol is to represent a living relationship. Relationships are not perceived; they are not objects. First and foremost they make up the milieu in which life exists." (*ibid.*, p. 298)

68 *Ibid.*

69 Alves, *ibid.*, p. 54.

70 Alves, "From Paradise to the Desert," p. 68.

71 See Alves, *ibid.*, p. 68, 74. Alves writes: "Our truth, then, is not the truth of absolute knowledge but the truth of faith; there is risk involved because faith cannot be separated from doubt. Absolute truth and truth's oneness are not a knowledge we possess but an eschatological horizon toward which we are moving." (*ibid.*, p.74).

"The great contribution that faith can make in the encounter with ideologies is its awareness that indeed 'now we see through a glass, darkly,' and that, whenever one claims to have seen reality face to face, one is bewitched by the desire for the absolute which lurks within men and cultures." Rubem A. Alves, "Marxism as the Guarantee of Faith," *Worldview* 16 (March 1973), pp. 17.

Also on Alves' reflections on Marx's and Freud's critique of religion see Rubem Alves, *What is Religion?* trans. Don Vinzant (Maryknoll, N.Y.: Orbis Books, 1984), espec. pp. 70–79; Rubem A. Alves, "Religion: Pathology or Search for Sanity," *Encounter* 36 (1975), pp. 1–9.

72 Rubem A. Alves, "Theology and the Liberation of Man," in *In Search of a Theology of Development,* p. 82

73   Alves, "Theology and the Liberation of Man," p. 81.

74   Alves writes: "I love the Calvinist fear of all kinds of idolatry. Idolatry—when someone says that God has been captured, when the Word is locked in a tomb and the dream becomes commandment." See Rubem Alves, "An Invitation to Dream," *The Ecumenical Review* 39 (1987), p. 61.

75   See Alves, "Theology and the Liberation of Man," p. 94.

Chapter 4

Christianity and Church

The focus of this chapter is the ecumenical character of liberation ecclesiology. For liberation theologians the model for the Church is community. The Church represents the eschatological community inserted into history, explicitly indicating God's activity in history in terms of the building up and manifestation of the Kingdom. The character and features of liberation ecclesiology distinguish it, as will see, from earlier understandings of ecclesiology which referred to the "marks" of the Church as a way of distinguishing the "true" from the "false" Church. In liberation ecclesiology the Church is essentially itself in its promotion of humanizaton and historical transformation in fidelity to the Word of God. Solidarity in the praxis of the Kingdom generates a deeply ecumenical ecclesiology.

Using main features in post-Reformation Roman Catholic and Protestant ecclesiologies as my point of departure, I chart some of the later revisions in both, prior to the emergence of liberation ecclesiology. I delineate then important features in the latter's retrieval of the Church as community and of praxis as the creator of community. The chapter is divided into three sections. Section One deals with the shift in post-Reformation Catholic ecclesiology from the more hierarchical and a-historical Church of Christendom to the communitarian and more historical understanding of the Church as the People of God. The importance of faith as service to the world in this ecclesiological shift and its reformulation in liberation ecclesiology as a hermeneutical option for the poor and oppressed is noted. Section Two traces the correlate changes in Protestant ecclesiology which led to a new understanding of ecclesiology as lived and active communitarian engagement with history.

Liberation ecclesiology builds on and reflects these crucial inter-religious developments in understanding. It retains the Reformers' understanding of the Church as a *"communio sanctorum,"* a holy community, revised now and inserted in history. It appropriates the recovery of eschatology through the contributions of Albert Schweitzer, Jürgen Moltmann, and the Protestant-Orthodox ecumenical movement. Section Three then elaborates on basic characteristics of the liberation configuration.

Post-Reformation Catholic Ecclesiology

The post-Reformation Roman Catholic understanding of the Church as a "perfect society" is abandoned in liberation ecclesiology. The latter defines the Church as the eschatological community that explicitly points to God's activity in history in terms of making life in the world more human. Vatican II also effectively abandoned the notion of the "perfect society" in its turn to a concept of Church as reflecting the joys and hopes of humankind and the world.[1] Vatican II effectively brought to an end the ecclesiology of Christendom and opened the way for a new type of Church, one with a pastoral presence and commission in the modern world. The Council's adoption of the eschatological category of "the signs of the times" as a hermeneutical key for understanding implications of faith and mission placed Catholic ecclesiology squarely in a historical-eschatological framework. According to Boff, the notion of the Church as a "perfect society" is linked to the Augustinian model of the Church as the City of God.[2] The relation of the Church as a "perfect society" to the world was separatist, indicating apartness from the world and from human activity. Under the influence of this schema the world existed for the Church, not the Church for the world. In Boff's opinion, there were no connections between the Church, the Kingdom, or the world. The Church was practically identified with the Kingdom since only within the Church did one find fulfilment. Only through the Church were salvation and the entire supernatural sphere made explicit. Apart from the world, the Church then duplicated many of the world's services. Thus there were Catholic schools, the Catholic press, Catholic colleges, Catholic universities, Catholic trade unions, and so on. This was how the presence of God was made explicit and guaranteed in the world.[3]

The dualism intrinsic to the ecclesiological notion of "perfect society" was also evident in the Church's hierarchical organization. The demarcation of priest/laity signified that the Church was not essentially a community but a hierarchy. Priestly life was confined to the interior life of the Church; the life of the laity was focused on and in the world. This, according to Boff, is the shape of classical ecclesiology; it takes only the hierarchy into account.[4] In it the faithful have only the right to receive. The bishops and priests control all religious "capital," produce the religious "goods," and the laity consume them. The model of the Church is monarchical, a feature common to the history of the Church.[5]

Diagrammatically the hierarchical/clerical ordering of the Church took shape in descending order as follows: GOD-CHRIST-APOSTLES-BISHOPS-PRIESTS.[6] According to Boff, immediately after Vatican II, the expression "Church as the People of God" was discovered, a tremendous change from the past. The change, however, did not affect the people. They wondered why it took the Church so long to discover something so obviously crucial and evident to anyone reading Christ's message.[7] In the mind of Vatican II, everything revolves around the People of God. Offices and services are subsequent to the notion of community. This is the fraternal and communitarian model.[8]

This ecclesiological shift which occurred at Vatican II not only retrieved the idea of the Church as a community of disciples, but it reestablished the relations between faith and human activity, the Church and the world. Prior to Vatican II, the movement known as Catholic Action played a crucial role in overcoming the dualism between the Church and the world. Essentially a bridge movement between the hierarchy and the laity, Catholic Action operated within the hierarchical model. It marked, however, the beginnings of a transition to the more communitarian configuration.

The designation itself, Catholic Action, in the accommodating sense of the term, was used to refer to any external action of a Catholic layperson inspired by his/her faith. In a stricter sense the term referred only to such action by lay persons/groups as mandated by local ordinaries. Here the term denoted a tightly structured organization that served as an arm of the hierarchy in lay life. Between these two senses were multiple types of organizations that were or were not classified as Catholic Action depending on the meaning of the concept prevailing in a particular country at a particular time.

Intrinsic to Catholic Action was lay involvement in terms of the practical working out of the demands of faith in history and the world. While theorists of the movement tended to be juridical and pedantic in their discussions, priests and lay persons engaged in the work itself, organized and developed their activities with much less rigidity due to their actual encounter with the needs of the world. In spite of being exposed to hierarchical control, Catholic Action was finally an influential movement which moved post-Reformation Catholic ecclesiology toward openness to the world. Under the influence of persons such as Cardinals Cardijn and Saliège, the movement contributed toward the recovery of Christian faith as praxis.

This development came to a head at Vatican II, with the promulgation of the Pastoral Constitution on the Church in the Modern World.[9] What the Council said of human nature as social or communal was also valid for the Church: "For the innermost nature of the human person is social; and if the human person does not enter into relations with others, he/she can neither love nor develop his/her gifts."[10]

In the Pastoral Constitution on the Church the Council expressed its communitarian self-understanding, brought an end to the ecclesiology of the "perfect society," and opened the door seeing/conceiving of itself in terms of service to humankind and the world. The ecclesiology of liberation theology adopted the Council's understanding of the essential servant nature of the Church—the essential mode of existence which witnesses to the presence and coming of the Kingdom. At these points where human existence is most vulnerable, this prophetic ecclesiology points to a future in which new possibilities exist for increased freedom and humanization.

Post-Reformation Protestant Ecclesiology

Ecclesiology in Post-Reformation Protestantism underwent revisions analogous to those in Roman Catholicism, in terms of a reinterpretation of the relation between the Church and the world, between faith and history. The Reformers' notion of the Church as a "*communio sanctorum*," a holy community, was set in greater dialectical relation with the world, history, and the Kingdom of God. Three important influences impinged on this development: the eschatological emphasis in the work of Albert Schweitzer, which effectively brought liberal theology to an end; the theology of hope movement, and Jürgen Moltmann's work; and the presence of Third World Christians in the global Protestant-Orthodox ecumenical movement. The result of this presence was a restructuring of the consciousness of the World Council of Churches (WCC) and a renewal of dynamism to contemporary Protestant ecclesiology.

The Reformers' understanding of the Church as community represented an ecclesiological shift away from the Roman Catholic notion of the "perfect society." Mainline Protestant ecclesiology still shared some of the features of the Catholic configuration. Luther, Zwingli, Calvin, and Cranmer were all magisterial reformers.[11] They carried out their reformatory work in alliance with the coercive power of the state, whether this was the magistrate, prince, town council, or, as in the case of England, the monarch himself.[12] The radical reformers, on the other hand, broke more decisively with the traditional concept of Christendom as an all-encompassing, unitary society.[13] Reformation traditions, however, retained overall some of the vestiges of Christendom. Later, their early liberative thrusts were brought under control and Christian faith itself used to subvert further attempts at total emancipation. Key teachings in the theologies of Luther and Calvin suffered this fate in some form.

Luther's key doctrine of the "priesthood of all believers" was an ecclesiological revision which re-captured the primitive understanding of the Church as community, not primarily as hierarchy. According to Timothy George, this was Luther's greatest contribution to ecclesiology.[14] In a word, it meant that "every Christian is someone else's priest, and we are all priests to one another."[15] With this development Luther broke decisively with the traditional division of the Church into two classes, clergy and laity.[16] Every Christian was a priest in virtue of his/her baptism, a member of a priesthood that derived directly from Christ: "We are priests as he is Priest, sons as he is Son, kings as he is King."[17] Priestly offices were therefore the common property of all Christians, not the special prerogative of a select caste of holy persons.[18] All Christians, according to Luther, enjoyed seven rights: to preach the Word of God, to baptize, to celebrate Holy Communion, to bear "the keys," to pray for others, to sacrifice, and to judge doctrine. This all rested on the biblical basis of 1 Peter 2:9 ("You are . . . a royal priesthood.") and Revelation 1:6 ("You have made them a Kingdom and priests.").[19]

The notion of the priesthood of all believers entailed a responsibility and a privilege, a service as well as a status. God, said Luther, has made us one body, one "cake." Our unity and equality in Christ are demonstrated by mutual love and care; just as we cannot give birth to ourselves, in the same way we cannot serve God by ourselves.[20] The explicit communitarian emphasis in Luther's ecclesiology was, however, checked by his theory of the two kingdoms, one a spiritual, operating through the word, and making for a righteousness geared to eternal life, the other a worldly government, also aimed at righteousness, but operating to make humans obedient through force and coercion.[21]

Luther's two-kingdom theory was dualistic and other-worldly, and the diremption between the two led to passivity and historical inertia. Luther, according George, elaborated his doctrine in opposition to two counter theories, medieval Catholicism and Anabaptism.[22] Against the Roman Catholic assertion of papal supremacy over secular rulers, Luther proclaimed the independence of the secular realm from clerical control.[23] Against Anabaptist religious separatism and literal interpretation of Jesus' injunction to non-resistance, Luther stressed the divine origin of the state, the limits of its power, and the basis for Christian participation in its coercive authority.[24]

Luther laid the foundations upon which Lutheranism later built its theory of Church-state relations, in which the Church tended to become a department of the state. The Church's prophetic voice in society was largely curtailed and muted.[25] Luther s doctrine of the two kingdoms, as Segundo wrote, was more than a political tool or the outcome of a specific political situation. It was bound up with central themes in his theology, not only justification by faith, but, in particular, the notion that glory belonged to God alone (soli Deo gloria). It had much to do with something Barth stressed before his death, namely, a rejection of the Catholic attempt to connect God and humankind, faith and good works. This turned faith, however, into a confident but essentially passive acceptance of God's plan for human destiny. Some Europeans in political theology, Segundo continued, would later use Luther's argument to counter any attempt to attribute to humans a historical causality in the construction of the kingdom.[26]

Historical passivity, inertia, and fixity in the understanding of human destiny and the construction of the kingdom revert directly to basic categories in Luther's ecclesiology. Despite its important retrievals and corrections of conceptual and practical abuses in the Catholic system, Lutheranism in the end became configured as an unavoidably static system. From its own common yet distinct starting points, Calvin's ecclesiology, with its humanistic thrust, ends in a similar configuration.

For Calvin, as for Luther, community was the key ecclesiological category. In Calvin the believing community was the locus of sanctification, not the society or the world.[27] The holy community thus represented the visible Church, "an agent of sanctification in the larger society," where every aspect of life was to be brought within the orbit of Christian purposes and Christian regulations.[28] Calvin's ecclesiology was more diverse in character than this representative significance. According to George, the diverse ecclesiological characterizations are only apparent when it is seen that Calvin never relaxes the visible/invisible tension in his view of the Church. One the one hand, for instance, the Church appeared to be in mortal danger. If false doctrines are allowed to spread, Calvin felt, they would "completely destroy the Church." At the same time, sub specie aeternitatis, human fickleness and unfaithfulness "cannot prevent God from preserving His Church to the end."[29]

For Calvin, the visible Church was a *corpus permixtum*, wheat and tares growing in the same field; the invisible Church included elect angels, Old Testament worthies, and assorted predestined souls who find themselves outside the "Lord's walled orchard." Indeed, the inscrutability of election, Calvin was reluctant to extend the title Church to select congregations still under Roman obedience. He was only partially concessive: "to the extent that some of the marks of the church remain, we do not impugn the existence of churches among them" (*Inst.* 4.2.12).

Because of pressures to develop a bipolar ecclesiology to preserve the Reformation vis-à-vis the Anabaptists and the Counter-Reformation, Calvin was constrained to identify the marks and character of the visible church. In addition to his images of community and the body of Christ, he added those of *Mater* (mother) and *Schola* (school).[30]

The church was Mother and School because believers were conceived in her womb, nourished at her breast, and enrolled as pupils in her school all the days of their lives (*Inst.* 4.4): "she brings them to new birth by the Word of God, educates and nourishes them all their life, strengthens them and finally leads them to complete perfection."[31] She is "God's school," the "pillar and ground of truth," instructing her students in "the study of a holy and perfect life."[32]

William J. Bouwsma comments that as "God's school," Calvin's church was more like a humanist academy than a school of theology. He imagined God looking over the shoulder of his pupils, watching "their gestures, walking, words, and everything else."[33]

While Luther and Lutheranism made it clear that what mattered in the Church was the living presence of Christ in His Word,[34] Calvin and Reformed theology treated with great breath the doctrine of the Church as a living and organically articulated community.[35] Both ecclesiologies were, however, Church-centered. Faith led not into the world but away from it. In the Barmen Theological Declaration of 1934 the Lutheran, Reformed, and United Churches of Germany re-affirmed the basic tenets of their common ecclesiology. The Church-centered emphases are clear; so is an a-historical orientation and uninvolvement in the world: The Christian Church is the community of brethren in which Jesus Christ acts presently as Lord in Word and Sacrament by the Holy Spirit. In the midst of the sinful world it is, as the Church of forgiven sinners, to witness by its faith and obedience, its message and its order, that it is His alone, that it loves and desires to live only by His consolation and by His orders, in expectation of His coming.[36]

In this declaration there is little concern to align faith and human activity in building God's Kingdom. The Church as a community living by the expectation of the Lord's coming has its gaze turned away from the concerns of humankind or the world, in an unwitting endorsement of existing conditions, whatever their character may be.

In its post-Reformation orientation Protestant theology has sought to retrieve the neglected historical-eschatological dimensions of its witness and character. Albert Schweitzer made an important contribution through his re-discovery of the apocalyptic and eschatological setting of Jesus' ministry.[37] So, as noted previously, did Moltmann and the theology of hope movement.[38] The Third Assembly of the World Council of Churches, meeting in New Delhi, India, in 1961 also significantly promoted the shift to history and humanization. According to Paul Lehmann, at New Delhi at least two actions of a paradigmatic kind were recorded. The first was the resolution which brought the International Missionary Council and the World Council of Churches into a common structural orbit.[39] The other was the admission into the World Council of the Russian Orthodox Church. As Lehmann put it:

> The paradigmatic character of the decisions taken at New Delhi exhibits the encounter between ideology and incarnation as the critical focus of the dynamics of the ecumenical situation today. The encounter between ideology and incarnation, moreover, is a critical contemporary ecumenical risk undertaken upon the initiative of the ecumenical movement itself.[40]

The shift at New Delhi revised the theological agenda by relocating it in dialogue with the modern world, in which the majority of human beings, who live in the Third World, are poor and oppressed. A new ecclesiology was bound to arise, based on this paradigmatic shift. For Lehmann this genesis arose from the Biblical imperative to risk one s very existence in order to find life. The ecumenical consequence of this imperative was plain: *Sancta ecclesia catholica et apostolica semper reformata semper reformanda.*[41]

Vatican II, which began a year later than New Delhi, in 1962, marked a similar watershed—with similar language and emphases—in Roman Catholic ecclesiology. Thus, the situation was effectively set for the emergence of a new ecumenical ecclesiology in which dialogue between faith and different ideologies would become part of the theological configuration. The school of Liberation Theology is the unique embodiment of this shift and *kairos*. In liberation ecclesiology the renewed communitarianism of Protestantism and Roman Catholicism is inserted in history and dialectically related to the Kingdom of God. Luther's understanding of faith as freedom, and Calvin's of sanctification as humanization have been historicized and freed of their individualistic dimensions. Faith also brings the Church into solidarity with humankind and its problems. Faith is the praxis of human historical transformation, and the Church the living sign of God's will to life, freedom, and humanization for all peoples.

The Lutheran two-kingdom theory is also abolished in Protestant liberation ecclesiology. No independent, supra-historical realm of being exists, divorced from human history and involvement.[42] In other words, this ecclesiology has adopted a unified theory of grace and history as its Roman Catholic counterpart has done. Across confessional lines therefore is an emergent ecclesiology, the concrete expression of a common historical-eschatological framework and a common task. In Bonino's understanding, a real inversion has taken place: the eschatological vocation of the Church, the call to witness to the coming Kingdom, takes precedence over a static identity with origins. It is a process of upheaval, accompanied by an ecclesial fluidity which makes traditional confessional criteria and institutional crystallizations largely irrelevant.

The most significant fact in contemporary Christianity is the increasing "condensation" of the Christian consciousness around foci which express a certain way of understanding the character and demands of the gospel and of Christian life.[43]

Segundo and Alves:
Ecumenical Ecclesiological Dimensions

For Segundo and Alves, as for liberationists generally, the Church is a historical yet transcendental community, which lives by the logic of the death and resurrection of Jesus.[44] This logic, as Alves put it, is a logic of creativity, determining the style and direction of all human interrelatedness.[45] In Segundo's words, the Church is a paschal community. Through Christ, God joined all human persons in solidarity and put love in everyone's hands as the divine instrument of salvation. This possibility of salvation is as vast and as ancient as humanity itself. It does not date from A.D. 1 or 30. Nor is it limited by the historical limits of the ecclesial community. Through Christ it reaches to all persons.[46]

For Segundo the revelation of this Christic plan suffuses all time.[47] The Christian is not the only person to enter into it, but is the one who through revelation and redemption knows it.[48]

The paschal community is also continually shaped by its participation in God's care for humankind. Thus the Church cannot opt out of history or dialogue with the world, but expresses its faith in obedient participation in God's will for the world. The Church's existence is the explicit expression that God is not transcendentally divorced from life, but is at work in the world and history through Jesus Christ. This is the substance of the Church's confession, worship, and proclamation.[49]

The Church: An Authentic Sacramental Community

Liberation ecclesiology interprets the life of the community of faith sacramentally. The community of faith is itself the sacrament of the Kingdom, that portion of humankind that has been drawn into the liberative and humanizing work of Jesus Christ. In Segundo's view, this is the primary sacrament, God's giving of God's self in Jesus Christ, the embodiment of the divine will to effect liberation and authentic humanization.[50]

Because of its relation to Jesus Christ the Church is an authentic sacramental community. It has received from Christ a ministry of reconciliation, which can only be mediated through praxis.[51] Praxis establishes the Church's identity as authentic sacrament. This means that the community is obliged to translate the plan revealed in Jesus Christ into the refashioning of history in terms of the Kingdom. As Segundo put it:

> The Church is, essentially and primarily, a sign. It has been placed here precisely and exclusively to pass on to humankind a certain signification, that is, a message, something that is to be grasped, comprehended, and incorporated to a greater or lesser degree into the fashioning of history in the world. If the very existence of the Church is meant to be leaven in the dough, salt in the meal, and light for all those who dwell in the human household, then the ecclesial community must accept the obligations that derive from its essential function.[52]

Sacraments in the Church shape and give creative expression to the life signified by the Church.[53] For Segundo they can also be the instrument of the recovery of the intrinsic unity of humanity, since, as community gestures, they associate us "with the perennial questions of humanity."[54] They can bring human beings into solidarity with one another, in terms of the common human questions human beings raise. Sacraments are thus avenues of consciousness raising. Having made possible a new human consciousness, they open the door for the mediation of praxis, in terms of providing.

The Church as the Embodiment of Messianic Creativity

The paschal logic that determines and shapes the Church makes it a community that embodies a messianic creativity. It is the sign and foretaste of the new humanity being created in Jesus Christ. Through the community, as Alves put it, Jesus "is inviting us to join the game of freedom and creativity, preconditions for human wholeness and social rebirth."[55] For Alves, the Bible answers the question of the historical shape of the creative act by pointing to a community of faith, the social reality where creativity is incarnated. The community is the objectification of the Spirit," *the place where the creative insight and the creative intention become creative power.*[56]

In Alves' ecclesiology, the Church, the embodiment of messianic creativity, is the locus of the recovery of authentic humanity in history. This recovery includes "the redemption of our bodies." This has very concrete application. It refers to things that have to do with society as a whole; it is not an individual affair: working conditions, salary, health, housing, water, yards, medical assistance, freedom to come and go, freedom from fear, knowing that we are not going to suffer violence, guarantee of a dignified old age, possibility of leisure time.[57]

The creative restoration implied in messianism is thus non-dualistic, refusing to separate the "body" from the "spirit." It restores to humankind what is absent from the totality of its existence. Messianism is also—by definition—extra-mural and non-parochial. It liberates the community for identification with the work of the Spirit wherever liberation and humanization need promotion.

The Church as Servant of Humankind

Liberation ecclesiology also discovers unity through service. It affirms that the Church was not instituted to save those within it but to perform a work of service for all humanity.[58] According to Segundo, "the obligation of the Church is none other than the obligation to love."[59] Whether the Christian does or does not perform the work of service depends on whether his/her goodwill gives way to exhaustion in broaching the radical questions of love.[60] God has revealed God's mystery to humankind so that it may know that love has to be fleshed out in history. On the day of final judgment, humankind will hear from its judge some such statement as: "Come, blessed of my Father, because I was hungry and your love had sufficient scope and hope to feed me."[61]

For Segundo the obligation to love, which defines the Church's commitment, has not only this spaciousness of scope. It includes an openness to encountering others in dialogue, as we explore the demands of the gospel and the questions raised by love. For Segundo, this dialogue is essential for what de Chardin called the "piloting of history." Vatican II demanded that we undergo a profound transformation that we may engage in dialogue.[62]

The Church is thus a community shaped by a mandate to serve and engage in the praxis of love. The service of humankind includes the guiding of history through the raising of questions in openness and dialogue. A special human solidarity is thus born of Christian servanthood, unifying all who work to promote God's Kingdom.

The Church as Unique: A Non-Mass-Produced Community

The Church in liberation ecclesiology is unique in that it is the expression of the birth of ultimate freedom in history. It is unique also as present wherever God's saving presence is at work in history in terms of promoting human transformation. Both this freedom and human transformation are gifts. The Church is therefore beyond being mass-produced. Alves speaks emphatically on this point:

> The Bible puts us in a bewildering situation. It acknowledges that the creative event erupts in history and assumes a social form, but it does not have any formula for duplicating it. The community cannot be mass-produced. We have no recipe for programming its growth or proliferation. But then what are we to do? The New Testament simply says: "Believe the good news"—somewhere, somehow it is happening. "Repent": throw away your old stethoscope and find a way of hearing the heartbeat of the future already pulsating in a community. And "be baptized": join it.[63]

The community of faith thus consists of persons who have heard God's good news of freedom and opted to participate in God's freedom movement. They have opted for discipleship in the building of God's regime in history. The praxis of this option brings them into solidarity with one another.

The Church as Heroic Minority Community

The minoritarian character of the Church has been particularly emphasized by Segundo, for whom "Christianity is supposed to be a leaven in the mass, a minority factor in itself."[64] The framework of Segundo's heroic minoritarian ecclesiology is historical-eschatological. It represents a radicalization of Vatican II's eschatological ecclesiology of the Church as the sacrament of the salvation of humankind.[65] In the modern world the Church is located in secular society, which does not assume ecclesiastical authority as its frame of reference. Being Christian is a voluntary option.

Only a small heroic minority can carry the Church's sign-bearing function to other opposed or pluralistic environments.[66]

Segundo's view is that the issue of minoritarian versus mass lines of conduct is crucial for all political processes as for Liberation Theology. Whether they realize it or not, theologies will be methodologically distinct, depending on the way in which they tend to relate the Christian message to either mass or minority ideas and lines of conduct.[67] Segundo's judgment is that a survey of the Christian Scriptures establishes a definite link between historical-political and biblical reflections on the issue of minoritarian versus mass behavior.[68] He claims that the following points are proved:

1. The exigencies of the gospel message are minority exigencies by their very nature and definition.
2. This does not point toward the maintenance of the interests of a small, self-enclosed group but rather toward the liberation of the humanity of the masses.
3. The liberation in question does not entail destroying the quantitative proportion existing between masses and minorities, since that remains equally operative in the Christian life. Still less does it entail reducing the exigencies of the gospel message to some minimal level so as to win the adhesion of the masses.
4. This minority effort among the masses is not meant to impose elitist standards on the latter, nor is it meant to construct a society based on minority exigencies. The aim is to create, for oneself and others, new forms of energy which will permit lines of conduct that are necessarily mechanized to serve as the basis for new and more creative possibilities of a minority character in each and every human being.[69]

The critical presuppositions underlying Segundo's minoritarian ecclesiology inhere in the very nature of the salvific claim of Christian faith. The Church cannot escape the radical demands of love. As the explicit locus of God's transformative action in history it is intrinsically called to costly discipleship in which minoritarian forms of behavior are obligatory. As the embodiment of messianic creativity in history the Church will be/must be counter-cultural, because it is the point at which the contradictions of history are being negated in terms of the Kingdom of God. For Segundo, if the Christian message is wholly identified with a particular cultural wisdom, the time would come when it would be reduced to a point where a creative return to its sources would be ruled out. The latter will cease to be normative, since they logically cannot be wholly identified with popular awareness as such.[70]

Segundo's understanding of the Church as heroic minority community presupposes that the Church has the capacity to be the agent of a new civilization founded on the Kingdom of God. Minoritarian ecclesiology coheres with the historical-eschatological framework proper to Liberation Theology. On the one hand, it expresses the fact that all persons are not willing or find it easy to embrace the costly demands of the gospel of freedom and love inherent in the Kingdom of God. On the other hand, it expresses the fact that the heroic community creates further possibilities for freedom and humanization in history. Minoritarian praxis opens up the present with its limited horizons to the creation of new spaces of liberation and civilization.

The Prophetic Mission of the Church to Liberation and the Historical Mediation of the Future

In liberation ecclesiology, as the Church commits itself to the humanizing praxis of faith, it acts prophetically in the world, especially as a "spokesperson for the wretched of the earth."[71] As with the ancient prophets of Israel, such activity on the part of the Church is a form of declaring: "Thus says the Lord."

Alves understands that the God of the Hebrew prophets was the God of the oppressed.[72] His prophets were those who dedicated themselves with unparalleled passion to announcing God's will and denouncing its subversion in prevailing conditions. Prophetic preaching was glued to the situation of the ordinary people. Key elements in that situation were the increasing centralization of the state in a few hands, the weakening of small, rural communities, and the diminishment of the small farmer due to heavy taxes, the growth of an urban capitalist class on the foundation of the estates the poor farmers had to sell. It was from this kind of situation the prophets arose as spokesmen for the poor.

> Everybody understood . . . when the prophets preached justice, that they were demanding an end to oppressive actions. Life and happiness must be returned to the poor, the suffering, the weak, the foreigners, the orphans and widows—in short, to all those who found themselves outside the spheres of wealth and power.[73]

A prophetic Church engages in what Dussel terms "the praxis of liberation,"[74] challenging unjust or oppressive systems constitutively, proclaiming and procreating a new order and a new structure.

Writing in a similar vein, Segundo states that the Church as the sacramental community of the prophet Jesus, has a mission to promote liberation in the world in the face of attempts by the State to endorse dehumanization. The Church would be faithful to her rationale and mission if she showed a clear commitment to collaborate in the work of authentic human development, or if she reacted firmly against political regimes that violate human beings. This image would take clearer form when people see Christians, as individuals and citizens, assuming a greater responsibility in this area.[75]

The image of the Church in Liberation Theology is therefore that of the sacrament or sign and agent of the world's transfiguration. This image corrects and transforms post-Reformation Catholic and Protestant ecclesiology by re-trieving and re-situating the Church's self-understanding in terms of its participation in the struggle for total humanization and restoration of history. Liberationist ecclesiology therefore shares in the divine communal, historical and eschatological vision through participation in God's suffering, the ultimate end of which is the transfiguration of all creation into the Kingdom or Temple of God. Indeed, this is another way of saying that God is Trinity.

Segundo and Alves, indeed liberation theologians as a whole, understand the Church's mission as the agent and sign of God's transfiguration of the world. In this concrete and historical praxis of the world's transfiguration Liberation Theology expresses its ecclesial ecumenicity and thus the basic unity of Christian existence and spirituality which Jesus Christ prayed for, and in which cause he died and rose. In the following chapter, then, I explore how this ecumenicity is displayed in the area of Christian existence or spirituality.

Notes

1 See *Pastoral Constitution on the Church in the Modern World*, Gaudium et Spes, Flannery, ed., secs. 1-3, pp. 903-05. The editorial footnote reads: "The Constitution is called 'pastoral' because, while resting on doctrinal principles, it seeks to set forth the relation of the Church to the world and to the man of today." *Gaudium et Spes*, p. 903. Consideration of the communitarian shift must keep in mind that the *Dogmatic Constitution on the Church, Vatican II, Lumen Gentium*, 21 November, 1964 in *Vatican Council II: The Conciliar and Post-Conciliar Documents*, Flannery, ed., secs. 18-30, pp. 369-388.

2 Leonardo Boff, *Church: Charism and Power. Liberation Theology and the Institutional Church*, trans. John W. Diercksmeier (New York: Crossroad, 1988), p. 3. Boff writes:

> Behind these practices lies an ecclesiology of the Church as a perfect society, parallel to that other society, the state. This is nothing more than a theological expedient for the affirmation of the Church's power, though it is seen as religious power. Religious power, here, is not understood by the Church as a way of understanding reality or as a 'spirit' in which to embrace all things; rather, religious power is concerned with a narrow aspect of reality controlled by the hierarchy.

3 Boff, *Charism and Power*, p. 3.

4 Boff, *ibid.*, p. 133.

5 Boff, *Church: Charism and Power.*

6 Boff, *ibid.* See also p. 133 where he diagrammatically lists three "marks" of the hierarchical Church: (1) Clericalism: a Church of the priests; (2) Imposing Church: anonymous, no information; institution, obedience to the laws; (3) Alienation: Church is only rites and sacraments; allied with the rich.

7 *Ibid.*

8 *Ibid.*

9 Dogmatic Constitution on the Church, *Lumen Gentium*, Flannery, ed., *Vatican Council II: The Conciliar and Post-Conciliar Documents*, pp. 350–432.

10 See *Gaudium et Spes*, sec. 12, in Flannery, *Vatican Council II: The Conciliar and Post-Conciliar Documents*, p. 913. I have paraphrased the translation in Flannery to make its language inclusive.

11 According to Timothy George, the term magisterial reformers was coined by George H. Williams, see George, *Theology of the Reformers*, p. 98.

12 *Ibid.*

13   *Ibid.*

14   George, *Theology of the Reformers*, p. 96.

15   *Ibid.*

16   *Ibid.*

17   *Ibid.*

18   *Ibid.*

19   George, *ibid.*, p. 96.

20   On Luther's definition of the Church as *communio sanctorum* see George, *ibid.*
      p. 96–97.

21   Quoted in George, *ibid.* See also, *ibid.*, p. 98.

22   George, *ibid.*, p. 99.

23   George, *ibid.*, p. 100.

24   George, *ibid.*

25   George, *ibid.*, p. 101.

26   Segundo, *Liberation of Theology*, p. 143. Segundo's reference to Niebuhr on
      this issue is very important. It helps to put the theology of Dietrich Bonhoeffer
      into perspective. It must be borne in mind that in their dialogue with European
      theologians Latin American theologians in search of their own theological *logos*
      have had to receive Barth in a critical way. Bonhoeffer, perhaps, has given them
      some more positive leads in dealing with their situation. Segundo's quotation
      from Niebuhr reads:

> Lutheranism, which in my opinion has the most profound religious insights on
> ultimate questions of human existence, has remained defective on problems of
> political and social morality, until the encounter with Hitler cured it of some of
> the most grievous errors: its doctrine of the "two realms"—the "realm of heaven"
> and the "realm of earth"; the one the realm of grace "where nothing is known
> except forgiveness and brotherly love" and the other the realm of "law" where
> "nothing is known except the law, the sword, the courts and chains." This
> might be a good description of the two dimensions of life and morals, but the
> fatal flaw in the doctrine of the two realms was that the one realm was that of
> private and the other of official morality. Politics, in short, was designed to
> maintain order in the sinful world. The purely negative function of the state
> was aggravated by an absolute religious sanction of its authority and the prohi-
> bition of all resistance. (See, Segundo, *ibid.*, p. 143.)

27   On this note Wilhelm Niesel defined Calvin's understanding of the Church as "a
      living organism, a communion of mutual service." In this sense the Church can be
      called a body. Niesel writes:

Christ does not hand over the gifts of His Spirit, which equips us for the service of others, to one individual. Each receives from Him, according to 1 Cor. 12, a special gift, enabling him to help to edify and influence the whole Church. By thus directing all the members to mutual service, the dominance of the Church by individuals which destroys the Church is excluded and Christ's own rule in the Church is confirmed. This does not mean that there is no superiority and subordination in the Church. It does mean that the brotherly solidarity and mutual help of the individual members must be maintained, if Christ is to be acknowledged as the One Head of the One Body which has many members.

See Wilhelm Niesel, *The Gospel and the Churches. A Comparison of Catholicism, Orthodoxy, and Protestantism.* trans. David Lewis (Philadel phia: The Westminster Press, 1962), p. 248.

Niesel also writes:

Using the gifts of grace available to them, our Reformed fathers sought to build up such a community of mutual service under the sole Headship of Christ, firmly knit together by mutual obligations, as a community Church which was able to withstand the storms of the Counter-Reformation.

Niesel, *ibid.*, p. 251. See also George, *ibid.*, pp. 235–36; Haro Höpfl, *The Christian Polity of John Calvin* (Cambridge: Cambridge University Press, 1982), p. 202.

28   George, *ibid.*, p. 236.

29   George, *ibid.*, pp. 237–38.

30   See Calvin, *Inst.* 4.1.1.

31   George, *ibid.*, p. 238.

32   George, *Theology of the Reformers.*

33   See William J. Bouwsma, *John Calvin: A Sixteenth Century Portrait* (New York, Oxford: Oxford University Press, 1988), p. 227.

34   Niesel, *Gospel and Churches*, p. 251.

35   *Ibid.*, p. 254.

36   Niesel, *Gospel and Churches*, p. 255. See also p. 256.

37   Schweitzer's thesis, according to A. T. Hanson, was that critical scholarship is bound by its own premises to give to the eschatological teaching of Jesus not a peripheral, but a central position. Jesus' eschatology is the key to a right understanding of his life, only by means of a consistent application of the eschatological category can we understand Jesus at all. See A. T. Hanson, "Eschatology," in *The Westminster Dictionary of Christian Theology*, pp. 183–86. See also Albert Schweitzer, *The Quest for the Historical Jesus* (London: T. & T. Black, 1926); on Schweitzer's theology see E. N. Mozley, *The Theology of Albert Schweitzer for Christian Inquirers* (Westport, Connecticut: Greenwood Press, 1974).

38   Jürgen Moltmann, *Theology of Hope: On the Ground and Implications of a Christian Eschatology* (New York: Harper & Row, 1967); *The Crucified God: The Cross as the Foundation and Criticism of Christian Theology* (New York: Harper & Row, 1974). For Alves' criticism of Moltmann see Alves, *Theology of Human Hope*, pp. 55–68. Alves' critique of Moltmann was dealt with in chapter two of this study. For Bonino's criticism of Moltmann see Bonino, *Doing Theology*, pp. 144–47, esp. pp. 144–45. For Gutiérrez's critique of Moltmann see Gutiérrez, *A Theology of Liberation*, pp. 11, 123–26. Gutiérrez writes: "The present is the praxis of liberation, in its deepest dimension it is pregnant with the future; hope must be an inherent part of our present commitment in history." Gutiérrez, *ibid.*, p. 11. For Moltmann's response to his Latin American critics, in what is known as the hope debate, see Jürgen Moltmann, "An Open Letter to José Míguez Bonino," (March 29, 1976) in *Liberation Theology: A Documentary History*, Alfred T. Hennelly, S.J., pp. 195–204. Moltmann's understanding of Alves' criticism was that his, Moltmann's theology of hope, was too transcendental in the definition of divine promise and too negative in the judgment of the present. See "Letter to Bonino," p. 197.

39   See Paul L. Lehmann, *Ideology and Incarnation: A Contemporary Ecumenical Risk, The Seventh Annual John Knox House Lecture, June 15th, 1962* (Geneva, Switzerland: John Knox House Association), p. 6. For Alves' indebtedness to this work of Lehmann, see Alves, *Theology of Human Hope*, pp. 27, 171 n.27. See also W. A. Visser 't Hooft, ed., *The New Delhi Report: The Third Assembly of the World Council of Churches 1961* (London: 1962); David P. Gaines, *The World Council of Churches: A Study of Its Background and History* (Peterborough, New Hampshire: Richard R. Smith, Noone House, 1966), p. 10007ff. The theme of the Assembly was "Jesus Christ the Light of the World." On the presence of the Roman Catholic observers at the Assembly, see Gaines, *ibid.*, pp. 1036ff.

40   Lehmann, *ibid.*, p. 11.

41   Lehmann, *Ideology and Incarnation*, pp. 6–7.

42   See Bonino, *Doing Theology*, p. 166.

43   Bonino, *Ibid.*, p. 156.

44   *Rebirth of Culture* (New York et al: Harper & Row, 1972), p. 199; also Alves, *Theology of Human Hope*, pp. 127–32.
        Liberation ecclesiology is based upon a theology of the logic of negation and non-identification. Conscientization and conversion is the process of discernment which allows the believer to identify and participate in the divine economy of salvation. To see God is to be taken up into God's redemptive plan. Alves and Segundo converge on this issue. Segundo places much emphasis on it in terms of his liberationist methodology defined in the hermeneutical circle.

45   Alves, *Tomorrow's Child*, p. 199.

46   Segundo, *The Community Called Church*, p. 11.

47   *Ibid.*

48   *Ibid.*

49   Bonino, *Doing Theology*, p. 171.

50   For further discussion on this issue in liberation ecclesiology see Bonino, *Doing Theology*, pp. 160–62.

51   Paul Lakeland comments on this aspect of Segundo's theology as follows:

> Segundo justifies his argument for the priority of the concrete historical struggle for justice by raising again the question of the mission of the church. If the mission of the church is to be for the world in the way he outlines it in *The Community Called Church,* then that mission is carried out in caring and service in solidarity with the world, in the world, not in the worshiping community. The sacramental life of the Church has instrumental significance. It is vitally important for Christians, the members of the ecclesial community, because it is their strength and support in the hard work of being the church in the world. Those who identify the sacramental life of the church as the "way to salvation" invert the proper order of things and abort the essentially missionary role of the church. Then the historical struggle becomes instrumental, secondary to the salvation obtained through participation in the sacramental life of the church.

See Paul Lakeland, *Theology and Critical Theory: The Discourse of the Church* (Nashville: Abingdon Press, 1990), p. 231.

Lakeland recognizes the fact that Segundo's theology, and Vatican II's, call for a total re-configuration of the Church as it is because of the turn to the world and the human situation. He writes:

> But if the church is rightly seen as for the world, not for itself, then it is lay ministry that is primary because lay ministry is more central to the essentially missionary role of the church. Ordained ministry as we understand it today is supportive or instrumental to lay ministry.

See Lakeland, *ibid.*, p. 232.

On Segundo's view on a contemporary liberationist approach to the Church's ministry of reconciliation, see Juan Luis Segundo, "Conversion and Reconciliation in the Perspective of Modern Liberation Theology," in *Signs of the Times,* Hennelly, ed., pp. 37–52.

52   Segundo, *The Community Called Church*, p. 81. The underlying functional question to Segundo's ecclesiology is: "What is the infinitesimal Christian community supposed to do within the vast community of mankind" (Segundo, *ibid.*, p. 4). Segundo argues that humankind was not made for the Church, the Church was made for humankind. The two ends of this scale must be balanced out. "This entity which is a specific and particular reality within mankind must have been created for humanity itself. This is the case, not the opposite. Humanity was not created to enter a particular reality which it overflows at every turn." (*Ibid.*, p. 6)

53   On Segundo's adoption and revision of Vatican II's understanding of the Church
      as sacrament, see Bonino, *Doing Theology*, p. 161.

54   See Juan Luis Segundo, *The Sacraments Today*, trans. John Drury, *A Theology
      for Artisans of a New Humanity*, Volume 4 (Maryknoll, N.Y.: Orbis Books,
      1974), p. 74.

55   See Rubem Alves, *Tomorrow's Child*, p. 99; also Rubem Alves, "Personal Whole-
      ness and Political Creativity: The Theology of Liberation and Pastoral Care,"
      Pastoral Psychology 26:2 (Winter, 1977), pp. 124–36.

56   Alves, *Tomorrow's Child*, ibid., p. 198. See also Alves, *Theology of Human
      Hope*, p. 143; Rubem Alves, *I Believe in the Resurrection of the Body,* trans. L.
      M. McCoy (Philadelphia: Fortress Press, 1986), p. 77.

57   Alves, *I Believe in the Resurrection of the Body*, p. 77.

58   Segundo, *The Community Called Church, p. 50.*

59   Segundo, *ibid.*, p. 32.

60   Segundo, *ibid.*, p. 50.

61   *Ibid.*

62   Segundo, *ibid.*, p. 60.

63   Alves, *Tomorrow's Child*, p. 199.

64   See Segundo, *The Community Called Church*, p. 216. Important works by
      Segundo on the minoritarian character of the Church include, *Masas y Minorias
      en la dialéctica divina de la liberación* (Buenos Aires: Editorial La Aurora, 1973);
      Funcion de la iglesia en la Realidad Rioplatense (Montevideo-Uruguay: Barreiro
      y Ramos S.A., 1962). For an Asian perspective on the minoritarian character of
      the Church which converges with Segundo's see Tissa Balasuriya, *Planetary
      Theology* (Maryknoll, NY: Orbis Books, 1984) p. 196. The issue is significant for
      the recovery of the Church's identity in a secular, plural, post-Christendom era.

65   On this see, for example, Bonino, *Doing Theology*, pp. 160, 161.

66   Bonino, *ibid.*, p. 80.

67   Segundo, *Liberation of Theology*, p. 228.

68   *Ibid.*

69   Segundo, *Liberation of Theology*, p. 231.

70   Segundo, *ibid.*, p. 236.

71   Rubem Alves, What is Religion?, trans. Don Vinzant (Maryknoll, NY: Orbis Books,
      1984), p. 71.

72   Alves, *ibid.*, pp. 70–79.

73   Alves, *What is Religion?*, p. 71. This is the classic way in which Latin American liberation theologians have appropriated the doctrine of justification by faith. See, for example, Elsa Támez, *Amnesty of Grace.*

74   Enrique Dussel, *Philosophy of Liberation*, trans. Aquilina Martinez and Christine Markovsky, (Maryknoll, NY: Orbis, 1985), p. 48.

75   Segundo, *The Community Called Church*, p. 97.

Chapter 5

Sacraments, Spirituality, and Christian Existence

So far this study has looked at ecumenical dimensions of Liberation Theology in the areas of grace and history, faith and historical transformation, and ecclesiology. This chapter looks at further dimensions as implied in and by all these important areas, namely, the sacramental and spiritual dimensions of Christian existence. The understanding of sacraments and spirituality in Liberation Theology continues the emancipatory thrust of the theological configuration so far explored, within the framework of history and eschatology. The dominant reality in that configuration is the Kingdom of God, and the terminus of the sacraments and the spiritual life is a transformed life, personally, socially and globally. The chapter is divided into two sections. In the first, which deals with sacraments, I explore how liberationists have gone beyond the received scholastic understanding in their sacramentology, not only in their basic revision of the category of "*ex opere operato,*" but also in the new, distinctive and ecumenically convergent lines of their sacramental reflection. Segundo and Alves, as we have seen throughout, in spite of differences in theological vocabulary, images, emphasis, and other influences from their respective traditions, show a substantive unity in theological perspective and conclusions.

Sacraments and the spiritual life in both theologians are distinguishable, not separable areas. The sacraments shape the Church for its mission as the sign of the world's salvation; they translate liberation into service.[1] Christian spirituality, the subject of the second section, is thus praxis rooted in and founded on sacramental nurture. This vision of spirituality also flows from the unified perspective on grace and nature. It is a way which signals that all dualisms are overcome. Liberation spirituality is also shaped by its contemporary context and *kairos*. Its chief preoccupation is not the sense of assurance over the forgiveness of sins or the feeling of awe before the glory of God, but the commitment or lived praxis of being God's collaborator in human and world transformation.[2] Spirituality, finally, like sacramentology, has necessary political and global and, not only, individual dimensions. It aims at a transformed humanity, a new human family, and a regeneration that extends to the entire cosmos.

Sacraments: Legacy, Renewal and Contention

Historically, Roman Catholicism has been a more sacramental tradition than Protestantism. The Reformation was in part a movement of reaction to sacramental abuse in Catholic ecclesiology.[3] With their emphasis on the Word of God, the Reformers sought to make sacramental theology more correlated with the Bible.[4] Within more recent times, significant movements of liturgical and sacramental reform have taken place in both communions, that have taken them, at least theoretically, beyond received divisions. The Roman Catholic form of this renewal came to a head at Vatican II with the promulgation of *Sacrosanctum Concilium*.[5] This has been paralleled by the Protestant *Baptism, Eucharist and Ministry*, which situated the sacraments within the framework of the Kingdom of God.[6] While the imperative of ecumenical rapprochement underlies these documents, sacramental theory and practice still remains an area of division between the communions, indicating how fixed the interpretive differences have been by the traditional understanding. The notion of "*ex opere operato*," that is, the sacraments are efficacious in their very performance, has been perhaps the chief area of controversy and disagreement. For Luther, the sacraments were not efficacious in their being celebrated (and in their conveyance of grace to anyone not in a state of mortal sin) but in their being believed. They were a Word of address from God, visible signs of divine intent, to be personally received, believed and appropriated.[7] For Calvin also, the sacraments were effective in proportion as we are helped by their ministry sometimes to foster, confirm, and increase the true knowledge of Christ in ourselves, at other times to possess him more fully and enjoy his riches. This happened when the sacraments were received in true faith. It was erroneous to think that there was a hidden power fastened to the sacraments by which of themselves they conferred the grace of the Holy Spirit upon us.[8] The sacraments were rather convenantal signs, by which the Lord sealed on human consciences the promises of God's goodwill toward us in order to sustain the weakness of our faith; we in turn attest our piety to God in the presence of the Lord through our obedient and committed reception.[9]

Liberation Theology has radically undercut the reasons for the traditional division between the communions by resituating the sacraments within the familiar overarching communal-historical-eschatological framework. The relation of sacrament to the Kingdom of God is essential to this relocation, as is the ecclesiological connection to the Church itself as sacrament of salvation and anticipation of final fulfillment.

Sacraments as Signs of Liberation and Eschatological Anticipation

For liberation theologians the sacraments are basic signs of God's liberative activity in history. They represent creedal or confessional summaries which declare God's saving acts, and create openness in life for the experience of God's continued and ultimate eschatological faithfulness. Sacraments are at the same time expressions of human gratitude to God for what God has done on behalf of human salvation, and of trust that God's love will never fail. They are also refreshment for human beings, lest they fall back into the abyss of despair, and they orient them to expect the ultimate victory of God's Kingdom. A brief reflective review of some of the sacraments underlines these liberative and anticipatory dimensions.

1. The Eucharist or Holy Communion is the central sacrament, declarative of the logic of the death and resurrection by which the Church lives. It represents the supreme expression of the dialectics of grace and history, fixing the life of the faith community within an historical-eschatological framework. The Eucharist is also the sacrament of the world's transformation, of authentic community and full humanity. It signifies that the community in which it is celebrated is a liberative community, which has tasted freedom and lives in anticipation of that time when Christ will wipe all tears from human faces and eyes. It is the supreme sacrament of human and ecumenical solidarity.

2. Baptism is the sacrament of personal conversion to God and to the Kingdom of love and justice announced by Jesus Christ. Individuals or (in infant baptism) sponsors express this commitment publicly. Baptism is more than an external rite or private ceremony, followed by the recording of names in the baptismal register.[10] A liberation approach critiques notions of baptism which deify bourgeois individualism at the expense of genuine participation in community. Baptism must be seen within the totality of Christian existence as the commitment to the pattern of life indicated by the paschal mystery, and to its dimensions of humanization and genuine freedom.

3. Penance includes the acknowledgment of debts in personal, communal and global dimensions. Tissa Balasuriya's question is very relevant here: "How is a people to be repaid for the loss of its dignity, culture, and freedom?"[11] In the light of colonization and imperialism, a related question is: "How can the slave ever be free?" Is the freedom of newly-emancipated peoples real? What debt shall be acknowledged and paid and by whom to those peoples who have been frustrated in the attempts at liberation and humanization?

4. Confirmation expresses the Christian commitment to world transformation. According to Balasuriya, this sacrament ordinarily has little significance in relation to the major questions of culture, liberation, and justice. When the apostles, on the other hand, received the Holy Spirit, they acted boldly to bring about a social transformation.[12] Confirmation should be seen as the Christian commitment to the communal creation of humanizing values. Sacramental interpretation should include exploration of a critical relation vis-à-vis individualism, materialism, sexism, racism, militarism, and nationalism.

Finally, a liberation understanding of the sacraments can in some contexts lead to collaboration in the creation of human communities with persons of other faiths, even with persons who do not belong to any faith, because the sacraments all express God's call to humankind to participate in the creation of a new heaven and a new earth. This collaboration will presume a respect for truth in other faiths and religions—in this way throwing further light on ecumenical dimensions in sacramental existence.[13]

The Liberation Critique of *"Ex Opere Operato"* Understanding and Magical Nature of the Sacraments

The traditional "*ex opere operato*" understanding of the sacraments has come under sustained critique in Liberation Theology. I will take Segundo's reflection on this subject as theologically representative of the liberation approach.[14] Later in the chapter I explicate, as I have done in previous chapters, some common meanings in his and Alves' understanding of sacramentology.

The expression, "*ex opere operato*," common to the Roman Catholic sacramental tradition, means that sacramental efficacy is guaranteed sheerly through sacramental performance and not on the moral character of the priest. A magical conception of the sacraments historically grew up around this understanding.[15]

The liberationist critique of the notion proceeds along several lines. A sheerly performative understanding is not in keeping with the modern and contemporary perspective in which human beings are free subjects of history. "*Ex opere operato*" also suggests a dualistic separation between faith and commitment. This leads by default to sacramentology in support of the status quo, rather than as symbolizing God's revolution for the world.

Segundo affirms that there is nothing intrinsically magical in the fact that the sacraments are efficacious channels of grace. A gift, accompanied by a gesture, is efficacious. No one would claim that a handshake which establishes and signifies friendship is magical.[16] In the controversy with Protestantism, Segundo maintains, the Council of Trent defined properly the "*ex opere operato*" efficacy of the sacraments. Trent wished to express two closely-linked realities: (1) that the sacramental act is not simply a reminder or commemoration of a gift really given by and from God; and (2) that God gives this gift unfailingly.[17]

In stressing these two points, Segundo argues, Trent did not introduce magical factors; it did, however, open the way for them. It seemed to suggest that God needed the sacraments in order to communicate grace. If, however, the sacraments are necessary, it is not because their absence would mean the absence of grace in the world. It is because without them the grace conferred would not be *signified*.[18] To insist on their character of signification is not to deny the aspect of efficaciousness; it is simply to indicate the why and wherefore of the reality of sacramentology itself. If a person receives the sacraments without comprehending their signification, that person would receive grace by virtue of his/her personal goodwill. It would not be Christian grace overcoming ignorance of the mystery.[19]

Segundo argues secondly that the infallible conferral of grace leaves room for some people, who seek to find a special privilege in the Church, to imagine that in the sacraments they have an infallible instrument of grace which they can manipulate. The sacraments are indeed infallible, given without strings attached and for good; but it does not cease to be a personal gesture calling for an equally human response. The infallible quality by degrees becomes linked up to the idea of the mechanical and the automatic, thence downgraded to the automatism and impersonal nature of the magical.[20] By way of correcting this sacramental understanding, Segundo proposes that we adopt a different perspective. We can construe the sacraments as personal gestures of Christ, the Savior of humanity; through these gestures he reveals his insertion and activity in everyone's life and summons us to join in the collaborative work of creation.

If this perspective becomes ordinarily normative, according to Segundo, we cross the uncrossable dividing line between magic and the sacraments.[21]

The sacraments issue a summons to participate with Jesus Christ in the conjoint project of the Kingdom. Through them the Church and Christian existence are shaped for mission in service of the world's salvation.[22] In Alves' theology sacramental theology issues in much the same perspectives, though with a different approach and from different angles.

Sacraments as Visible Signs of Absence and Symbols of Return

Alves concurs with Segundo in regarding the sacraments as signs of liberation and eschatological anticipation. They are signs of absence and symbols of return, the nostalgia of our souls. Alves offers a general definition of a sacrament in *I Believe in the Resurrection of the Body*:

> When things awaken longing remembrance and cause the memory of love and the desire for return to grow in the heart, we say, that they are sacraments. This is a sacrament: visible signs of absence, symbols which make us think about return. Like what happened with Jesus who, just before his departure, carried out a memorial of longing remembrance and of waiting.[23]

Sacraments as visible signs of absence and symbols of return shape the Church's memory so that it continually keeps the present open for the fullness of the coming of the Kingdom. The Church's memory must be critical if it is to continue to be a historical-eschatological community. Critical memory creates history; it mediates and makes imaginatively and really present the future through the power of longing remembrance.

Longing remembrance centers around Jesus Christ in a very special way in the Eucharist. According to Alves, Jesus "became transparent and we began to see the world through him."[24] "Without transparency there is no eucharist."[25] In its eucharistic practice the community of faith expresses its distinctive beliefs.

The community's memory of Jesus, celebrated publicly in the Eucharist, functions as the antithesis and corrective of the human tendency to amnesia and denial, the preference for superficiality and instant gratification. In its commemoration of Jesus the community remembers the love of God He reveals. It recalls, celebrates, and participates in God's recovery of lost humanity in Him. To receive the Eucharist in faith is thus to join in the divine protest and activity against dehumanization.

The eucharist, the witness of human solidarity and hope, points to the definitive exodus in which Jesus Christ is the resurrected Head of the New Humanity. It is the gift and promise of complete and integral liberation, the pledge that not even death, the final enemy, is able to separate humankind from the love of God and the solidarity of one another.

Sacraments as Anticipations of the Values of the Future

The sacraments introduce into human history those values upon which the final eschatological completion is founded. Through the sacraments, and the life they fashion, the ethics of the kingdom are incarnated in history. The desire, vision, and values necessary for the restoration of history to its primordial unity are revealed through sacraments.

> Parable of what the Church is: those who have already experienced the aperitif of a new world. Paul doesn't talk about aperitif. He talks about "first fruits." But who among us, so far from the miracles of the trees that give fruit, understands what he is trying to say? Imagine that before the abundance of flowers and fruits, nature should send us, beforehand, samples of that which is to come. First fruits, messengers. And so we can, in anticipation, taste the good taste of that which is coming. They don't nourish us. They awaken the appetite. They make us desire, with more intensity. That's the way it is, too, with the aperitif which does not satisfy hunger but prepares the body for the food. It's like the caress which prepares the bodies for the union of the bodies in love.[26]

As aperitifs, samples, and messengers of the Kingdom, sacraments enshrine the values on which the economy of the Kingdom is built. The Church embraces these values in fidelity to Christ. The values are not for the Church alone, but for all humankind. The mission of the Church is to make these aperitifs transparent to/for the entire human community.

This imperative of responsibility stems from the fact that through the sacraments we are those "who were caressed by Someone from the future." Because we have been so caressed, "everything has changed."[27] Then, just as a woman who discovers she is pregnant, begins anticipatedly to incarnate her child, so the Church is the community in which the future will take shape. It is the first fruits, the caress of the future of the Kingdom.[28]

From this caress arises anticipatedly a vision of "our bodies become totally free. Free of everything that causes suffering."[29] The Church exults in this vision of liberation—and is moved to serve the world and fulfill the demands of the Kingdom. Possessing what it hopes, it lives to witness to and be servant of that hope.

(We will be) free of chains, of fear. The eyes will no longer pierce, and none of us will have to hide, from anyone, either the nudity of our soul, or the nudity of the body. Free for truth, for beauty, for love . . . Possessed by the future, we will try to bring to life, in the present, that which was given to us in hope. And this community of visionaries, of exiles, of pilgrims, of uprooted trees, will serve the world, in their own life, in sacraments of the Kingdom that is drawing near.[30]

Sacraments in Segundo as Expressions of Truth, Commitment to History, and Signified Grace

In Segundo sacramental theology is correlated with his emphasis that faith should not be divorced from life and its commitment. Christian faith ultimately is a creative praxis verified by its historical efficacy. The principle of efficacy also applies to the sacraments.

Segundo explicates the issue of sacramental efficacy in another way. The sacraments are expressions of truth and commitment to history. To clarify this assertion, Segundo uses Alves' definition of truth as the solutions people arrive at in order to effect their liberation and humanization in history.[31] Truth is a matter of orthopraxis, and the truths conveyed by the sacraments are thus efficacious truths. They realize human transformation.

As symbolic and effective of such human possibility and transformation, sacraments are also signified grace. They make manifest the presence in the world of the power of God to liberate and transform.

Segundo, like Alves, links his sacramental reflection importantly to the Eucharist and the paschal mystery it commemorates. The sacraments are, for him, a vehicle for the responsibility of applying to history and historical events the paschal mystery, which is the basic Christian liberative schema.[32]

This linkage serves to underline the liberative significance of the Eucharist itself, the other sacraments, and the Church which celebrates them. Through such celebration a community is created that makes a particular message transparent, that is, the good news of liberative love. This love (mirrored on the logic of the paschal mystery) keeps individuals, communities, and the world from being turned in on themselves, and turned outwards to greater levels of solidarity. The sacraments, the Eucharist in particular, thus also make the Church what it is, God's vehicle for God's message of liberation, and the empowerment of a community to accomplish this mission creatively. Through the sacraments God grants and signifies to the community the grace which constitutes it in its being and mission within the larger human family.[33]

The Sacraments as Communitarian Fashioning
of the Church and Pedagogy for Mission

To elaborate further on the foregoing section, Segundo asserts that a visible, concrete community life is a basic exigency of the Christian life rather than an ideal of perfection. The sacraments fashion this community life of the Church.

The Church as community means an association of mutual aid in which persons practice the dimensions of real encounter and love, not simply by reading or reflecting, but by proffering real, concrete help.[34] The mutual aid of the community, however, is not its intrinsic justification; mission is not confined to the ambit of the community only. If no wider goal existed, the community would rapidly run down,[35] and in fact cease to be a Christian community.[36] The sacraments thus both fashion *and* amplify the community and missionary life of the Church.

In terms of mission also, the sacraments situate the Church in an essentially conflictual history. The seven sacraments, Segundo argues, constitute a locus for struggle and resolution in this history.[37] When taken in isolation from a creative community, they entail a basic a-temporality and routineness. Within such a community, however, they bring the solidarity of a common endeavor and quest to people living through different, even radically opposed situations and challenges. What they ensure is that each basic community will not escape into a facile and uncritical unanimity in its response to a specific matter of urgency.[38]

The nature of the sacraments as conflictually situated directly indicates the Church's prophetic function, which entails sacrifice. Segundo notes, for instance, in this connection Camilio Torres who never ceased to find the sacraments themselves meaningful.[39] What Torres found meaningless was the notion of continuing to dole out sacraments to Christians who were evidently closed to love, insensitive to justice, and unfeeling toward the poverty and anguish of their dispossessed fellows.[40]

The sacraments must also be consciousness-raising, if they are to perform their function of teaching the Church its course of action in fidelity to its mission. Segundo here expresses his indebtedness to the Brazilian thinker, Paulo Freire. The sacraments must lead the community from deformation to information, passivity to activeness, object to subject status, false to authentic consciousness.

Spirituality: Roman Catholic and
Protestant Historical Deficiencies

Catholic Liberation Theology has revised the understanding of spirituality dominant since the Counter-Reformation by stressing spirituality as the lived praxis of faith in solidarity with the world. This emphasis came into its own with Vatican II's abandonment of a two-planes theology, and the adoption of a unified theology of grace. The opposition between the "natural" and the "supernatural" levels of existence was abandoned, and the way opened for construing all existence as graced and called to communion and friendship with God.

Looking back on this fundamental shift in spiritual perspective, Segundo notes the pejorative connotation which the term "spirituality" had taken on in some circles as stemming from this theoretical and practical theological separation (opposition) between the two planes. On the higher plane people discussed "supernatural" or "eternal" problems; the lower plane was the sphere of purely "temporal" or "natural" affairs. The spirituality generated by the new theology now "throws a new light on everything, manifests God's design for humanity's total vocation, and . . . directs us to fully human solutions to historical problems."[41]

Protestant liberationists have also revised the standing of spirituality in post-Reformation Protestantism through their radical turn to the world and history. According to Gordon S. Wakefield, attempts have been made to maintain that "spirituality" is a phenomenon more Roman Catholic than Protestant, and that the latter has kept pure a biblical and Pauline understanding in contrast with the Catholic tendency to spiritual syncretism.[42] John Dillenberger and Claude Welch have argued, however, that the great temptation in Protestantism has been not the idolatry of particular religious forms, but the opposite, that is, the lack of concern for all forms and the consequent weakening of the sense of the sacred. A religious perspective, they claim, which rejects all finite claims to ultimacy runs the risk of failing to see that the ultimate is known only through finite vehicles.[43] In an analogous vein Moltmann has maintained that the Protestant reluctance to develop forms of spirituality, as keeping the human encounter with God free and spontaneous, can be a substitute for avoiding the necessity of a real political liberation in the world.[44]

The turn of Protestant liberationists to articulation of a Christian spirituality of praxis accomplishes two things. It explicitly inserts spirituality in Protestant theology and culture, and corrects a "lacuna" in the Reformation theological legacy. According to Timothy George, none of the Reformers took over the mystical traditions of the medieval period without qualification, but their theologies cannot be understood without the intense craving for the divine immediacy which characterized that vision.[45]

In George's view, the absence of mystic immediacy left Reformation spirituality suspended between a lost transcendence on the one hand, and a lack of radical historicality (and eschatology) on the other. This dualist bifurcation is apparent in Luther's two-kingdom doctrine. The historical need in post-Reformation Protestantism became the need for an approach that considered transcendence and history in serious and dialectical relation, the theological mode espoused by Protestant and Catholic liberationists.

Spirituality in Alves as a Hopeful, Counter-Cultural Vision of the Future

Alves' book, *Tomorrow's Child*, is to his spirituality what *I Believe in the Resurrection of the Body* is to his sacramental theology.[46] In it he argues that Christian existence is subversive of the present world/order/ *oikoumene* through its counter-cultural vision of an alternative future. Like the community of Israel, the early Christian community was counter-cultural, or more accurately, an underground counter-culture. It was persecuted ruthlessly because the dominant powers of the time saw it as a subversive social reality. Its values in the long run implied an undermining of the very foundations of the Roman Empire.[47]

Christianity's alternative vision, in Alves' view, releases human persons for participation in mediating the Kingdom of God. To despair of the possibility of the Kingdom's coming is to sin. Alves here recalls Bultmann, to the effect that sin is the fear of the future, which forestalls its coming.[48] Hope on the other hand provides a perspective that makes transformation possible. Even tragedies are not seen as ultimate.[49] Even there, promise and hope remain. Human beings will keep on dying for their visions, and their suffering and death will be the seed from which a resurrected future emerges.[50]

The spirituality of this vision of hope is not an opiate, but a subversion of the present order, the anticipation in imagination of a different possibility.

Spirituality as Suffering with the Oppressed

Spirituality in Alves also implies identification with the struggles and suffering of the oppressed. This dimension is beautifully captured in one of the prayers in *The Resurrection of the Body*:

We thank you for this strange, terrible, marvelous power of our body, power which makes it spiritual and image of your love, power to feel pity and compassion, so that the sufferings of other bodies are felt as if they were our own. We suffer with those who suffer and know that when we suffer we are not alone. With this body we live the fraternity of love. We want you to enrich us, freeing us from the narrow limits of our skin, making our body fill out, to feel the pain of others. And so—open to joy and in solidarity in suffering, expressions of hope and love— may our bodies be living manifestations of the Body of Christ, destiny of the universe. Amen.[51]

The alternative future hoped in by liberation spirituality does not come without travail. Meanwhile, the poor struggle with the realities of poverty and oppression. A Christian spirituality enters into this suffering in solidarity, longing and commitment: solidarity with the pains of those suffering, longing for an order which annuls the present, and committed to working for the emergence of that order.

Spirituality as Freedom and Carnival

Human imagination also plays an important role in Alves' spirituality, not only as subversive of the present, and as making for empathy with the pains of the suffering, but as aligned with freedom and play. This is his spirituality's utopian dimension, where it envisages the freedom and amplitude announced by the Kingdom. The vision is of a world from which cruelty is banished; there is an end to torture and beatings, hunger, the exploitation of the weak; truth and justice rule; the old are afraid to walk the streets; all armaments are destroyed in a huge bonfire. This is the carnival of all humankind.[52]

As a Brazilian, Alves is familiar with the phenomenon of carnival, with its celebration of the power of creativity and the festive imagination. Carnival in settings of former slavery or repressed culture (like Brazil) also means more. It is the popular expression of a desire for an alternative concrete totality, a celebration of energy, hope, and spiritual vitality. A carnival of humanity is thus Alves' code expression for a vision of a world transformed, a better world and society for everyone, a complete re-configuration of reality, in short, a desire to enjoy and participate in the plenitude of the Kingdom, it is the vision of a new heaven and new earth.

Spirituality in Segundo as a Creative/
Prophetic Way of Liberation and Pedagogy

Spirituality in Segundo is grounded in the Pauline axiom that the fundamental capacity that should be operative in the community is that of love. There is, however, a hierarchy of capabilities for the concrete implementation of love, the most important of which is the prophetic. The prophet looks into events, discerns their deeper, underlying meaning, and relates it to God's plan:

> Today the community gathers almost exclusively in terms of the sacramental realm. But Paul says: "So if the whole congregation is assembled and all are using the 'strange tongues' of ecstasy, and some uninstructed persons or unbelievers should enter, will they not think you are mad? But if all are uttering prophecies, the visitor . . . hears from everyone something that searches his conscience and brings conviction, and the secrets of his heart are laid bare. So he will fall down and worship God, crying: "God is certainly among you!" (1 Cor 14: 23-25).[53]

Prophetic spirituality concretizes the divine plan of love in history, promoting the conversion the plan requires and the need for personal and communal transformation according to its demands.

Spirituality as Mature and Authentic Personhood

In Segundo's view, a Christian spirituality of liberation must also be in critical correlation with the profound questions posed by human experience. Every profound experience opens out into a question of the meaning of existence.[54] This most natural human query is charged with wonder and anguish: Who are we? What are we? Liberation spirituality must therefore grasp us at our existential core and provide authentic answers to our ultimate concern.

This question, which takes us to the issue of the meaning of our existence, becomes deep and real at the end of all pathways. We come at that point to a costly and difficult task, without skipping steps, or lying, or giving in to facile solutions, or ideologies, or escapist strategies. We can refuse the risk of thinking or latch on to religion as insurance for the beyond. The difficult road is to live deeply, to take existence into our own hands, to make ourselves consciously and deliberately. This is the biblical narrow gate that leads us always to the profound questions: Who am I? Who are we?[55]

A liberationist spirituality is thus heuristic, leading the human subject progressively into personal liberative truth. For Segundo the epistemological process implied here causes both believer and unbeliever to traverse the same road, forcing upon both the same obligations of authenticity and communication. Speech and language go through a deep ascesis, before they become an authentic *logos*.[56] At this point the believer can proclaim the good news. Without growth in authenticity and without the experience of communication, the proclamation of faith runs the perennial risk of becoming an ideology or a myth unacceptable to honest seekers.[57]

Spirituality as Solidarity in Oppression and Openness to an Alternative Future

An authentic liberation spirituality also plumbs the depths of human experience in situations of oppression and lives in solidarity with the oppressed. From another perspective such solidarity is an imperative of living the logic of the paschal mystery, which is the supreme mystery of love. The human commitment of solidarity is thus seen by Segundo as theologically supported and grounded in the revelation of God's love in Jesus' life and death. Segundo's liberationist spirituality is understandable in terms of his project of revising Ignatian spirituality, centered in the Exercises, in light of Vatican II, Medellín and the exigencies of Latin America.[58]

Segundo advocates an active, project-oriented spirituality, one which is historically oriented in terms of co-operating with God in building up the Kingdom in the world. It is not a passive, test, contemplative type spirituality. It is a spirituality that points to the total re-configuration of all reality according to the constitution of the Kingdom of God as revealed in the ministry of Jesus Christ. It is the spirituality of those who are God's co-workers in renewing humankind and creation from the point where they are most vulnerable. According to Segundo, if I envisage God as a political figure who proposes to establish a kingdom (this is the image that Jesus used in speaking of his Father); if I view this figure as not primarily preoccupied with who the good and the wicked are, but starts with who suffer the most, or who are the marginalized, most prevented from realizing their humanity; if I begin with these presuppositions, then I will read the Gospel to see what it tells me of those persons to whom and with whom I make my commitment.[59]

Spirituality thus involves solidarity with the poor and the oppressed. It is in solidarity with the poor, those most oppressed, that one manifests the spirituality of the Kingdom of God. This is the classic expression that one trusts in the divine project and is radically open to the future to which it points. One demonstrates one's confidence in the project by committing one's self to it in love and trust. To love, Segundo observes, is to entrust something crucial of ourselves to others, to share a common project. When, therefore, we say that God is love, we mean that God makes human beings indispensable collaborators in a project of great importance both to God and to human beings.[60]

Moreover, comments Segundo, the conception of a historical project common to both God and the human being was absent from the theology of the Counter-Reformation as it was from that of the Reformation.[61] The spirituality of solidarity with the oppressed and trust and openness to the future which Segundo is articulating is thus ecumenical in that it transcends post-Reformation Catholic and Protestant attitudes to spirituality. It is also ecumenical in that its effectiveness lies in its opening of a common future for all humankind beginning with the most oppressed. It is the spirituality of the historical-eschatological Kingdom of God: The criterion of belonging to this kingdom is revealed in the one God will use to judge the nations (Matt. 25:31). All that is done for the least of our brothers and sisters immediately affects God.[62]

Segundo vividly brings out the ecumenicity of this historical-eschatological spirituality when he writes:

> Suddenly we see that the fact that God is love, a fact derived from Christology, leaves behind any conception of human existence as a *test*. It plants us before a common human and divine *project* that is unfolding in the history of human beings and their dire needs.[63]

This is the ecumenical spirituality that shoulders the cause of the poor and the oppressed and offers creative collaboration in conspiring with, breathing with God in the establishment of God's Rule in the world. This is the nature of the spirituality that is based on God's revelation in Jesus Christ.

As with Alves' vision, solidarity with the oppressed in Segundo also looks to the emergence of an alternative order, a re-configuration of reality. It is not only protest but affirmation and hope. It is that spirituality that ever works for and prays that God's Kingdom may come on earth as it is in heaven. Liberation Theology, in its spirituality is also ecumenical in its bearing of the cause of Christ's Kingdom in history.

Notes

1   See Pastoral Constitution on the Church in the Modern World, *Gaudium et Spes,*
    Vatican II: Conciliar and Post-Conciliar Documents, ed. Flannery, sec. 44.
    p. 947:

> Whether it aids the world or whether it benefits from it, the Church has but one
> sole purpose—that the Kingdom of God may come and the salvation of the
> human race may be accomplished. Every benefit the people of God can confer
> on mankind during its earthly pilgrimage is rooted in the Church's being 'the
> universal sacrament of salvation;' at once manifesting and actualizing the mys-
> tery of God's love for men.

    Also see, *The Dogmatic Constitution on the Church, Lumen Gentium, Vatican
    II: Conciliar and Post-Conciliar Documents,* ch. 7, sec. 48, p. 407: ". . . he
    sent his life-giving Spirit upon his disciples and through him set up his Body
    which is the Church as the Universal sacrament of salvation."

2   See George, *Theology of the Reformers,* p. 320. Luther writes:

> For who would not simply stand awe-struck before the forgiveness of sins and
> life everlasting rather than seeking after them, once he had weighed properly
> the magnitude of the blessings which come through them, namely, to have
> God as father, to be his son and heir of all his good! See Luther, "Babylonian
> Captivity of the Church," in *Martin Luther's Basic Theological Writings,* Ed.
> Lull, p. 301.

3   See Luther, "Babylonian Captivity of the Church," *Martin Luther's Basic Theo-
    logical Writings,* Ed. Lull, p. 305.

4   This attempt on the part of the Reformers led to their unanimous critique of an
    "*ex opere operato*" understanding of the sacraments. The Reformers understood
    the sacraments as signs of God's promises to humankind which were to be re-
    ceived by faith. See Jürgen Moltmann, *Theology of Hope: On the Ground and
    Implications of a Christian Eschatology,* p. 44:

> The correlate of faith is for the Reformers not an idea of revelation, but is
> expressly described by them as the *promissio dei: fides et promissio sunt
> correlativa.* Faith is called to life by promise and is therefore essentially hope,
> confidence, trust in the God who will not lie but will remain faithful to his
> promise. For the Reformers, indeed, the gospel is identical with *promissio.*

    See also *Martin Luther's Basic Theological Writings,* ed. Lull, p. 257 n. 39:

> ". . . The sacrament is not a good work or sacrifice on the part of man, but
> a testament or promise on the part of God, to be received by man in faith—not
> an *officium* but a *beneficium.*"

5   See *The Constitution on the Sacred Liturgy, Sacrosanctum Conculium*, 4 December, 1963 in *Vatican Council II: Conciliar and Post-Conciliar Doc uments*, Flannery, pp. 1–270.

6   *Baptism, Eucharist and Ministry*, Faith and Order Paper No. 111 (Geneva: World Council of Churches, 1982, 22d. Printing, July, 1988). This document explicitly sets the sacraments in a historical-eschatological framework.

7   See Martin Luther, "The Babylonian Captivity of the Church (1520)," p. 293 n.84, 85 in *Martin Luther Basic Theological Writings*, Ed. Lull, pp. 267–313; "Sermon on Preparation for Dying (1519)," *ibid.*, pp. 638–654; "A Treatise Concerning the Blessed Sacrament (1519)," *ibid.*; *Luther's Basic Theological Writings*, p. 257 n. 39:

> Thus the Scholastics all agreed that the sacraments imparted grace *ex opere operato*. According to Duns Scotus and Gabriel Biel the necessity of faith is expressly denied and a purely passive receptivity is held to be sufficient. Intended originally to affirm that the power and effect of the sacrament are caused not by any disposition on man's part but solely by God and the sufferings of Christ, the concept *ex opere operato* thus ultimately came to mean that the proper disposition on the part of the recipient need not be one of positive faith but of merely negative passivity. It was this latest, fullest, and perhaps logical development of the Scholastic view that Luther is attacking.

Lull commented (*ibid.*) that ultimately, Luther's solution lay not in the preference for *operantis* over *operatum* but in the rejection of the opus altogether. The sacrament is not a work.

8   Calvin: *Institutes of the Christian Religion*, Vol. 2, McNeil and Battles, p. 1291.

9   Calvin, *ibid.*, McNeil and Battles, p. 1277.

10   Balasuriya, *Planetary Theology*, p. 232.

11   Balasuriya, *ibid.*, p. 234.

12   Balasuriya, *Planetary Theology*.

13   Balasuriya, *ibid.*, p. 237.

14   Segundo's major work on the sacraments is *The Sacraments Today*. For Alves it is *I Believe in the Resurrection of the Body*.

15   Segundo's definition of magic is "Magical actions are different from ordinary actions in two respects, insofar as their outcome is concerned. Firstly, in terms of expected efficacy, there is no normal relationship between the means employed and the outcome. Secondly, the outcome is not dependent on whim; it is tied by a superhuman power to certain fixed ritual gestures or words." Segundo, *Sacraments*, p. 6.

16 Segundo, *The Community Called Church*, p. 39.

17 *Ibid.* Segundo's italics.

18 Segundo, *ibid.*, p. 39. Segundo's italics.

19 Segundo, *The Community Called Church*, p. 39.

20 *Ibid.*

21 *Ibid.*

22 See Segundo, *The Sacraments Today*, pp. 42–67.

23 Alves, *I Believe in the Resurrection of the Body*, p. 13. See also Rubem A. Alves, "Theo-poetics: Longing and Liberation," in Lorine M. Getz, Ruy O. Costa, eds., *Struggles for Solidarity: Liberation Theologies in Tension* (Minneapolis: Fortress Press, 1992), p. 168.

24 Alves, *I Believe in the Resurrection of the Body*, p. 25.

25 *Ibid.*

26 Alves, *The Resurrection of the Body*, pp. 74–75.

27 Alves, *ibid.*, p. 75.

28 Alves, *ibid.* Alves does not equate the Church with the Kingdom. The caress calls the Church into alignment with the Kingdom but the two are identical.

29 Alves, *I Believe in the Resurrection of the Body*, p. 76.

30 *Ibid.* On the issue of nudity and community in liberation theology and philosophy see also Enrique Dussel, *Philosophy of Liberation*, pp. 78–87.

31 Segundo asks: "Is it possible for the truth that derives from faith to form a realm of its own, the realm of truth-in-itself, when faith and those other terms are subject to the test of historical efficacy? Must we not end up by defining truth as Rubem Alves does, when he says it is "the name given by an historical community to those acts which were, are, and will be efficacious for man's liberation?" See Segundo, *The Sacraments Today*, p. 54; p. 66 n.5.

32 Segundo, *The Sacraments Today*, p. 97.

33 Segundo, *ibid.*, p. 99.

34 Segundo, *Sacraments Today*, p. 35.

35 Segundo, *ibid.* p. 35.

36 *Ibid.*

37 Segundo, *ibid.* p. 60.

38 Segundo, *The Sacraments Today*, p. 60.

39 Segundo, *ibid.*, p. 38.

40   *Ibid.*

41   Juan Luis Segundo, *Christ of the Ignatian Exercises*, p. 126; also *Gaudium et Spes*, sec. 11, Flannery, *Vatican II: Conciliar and Post-Conciliar Documents*, p. 912.

42   See Gordon S. Wakefield, "Spirituality," in Richardson and Bowden, eds., *The Westminster Dictionary of Christian Theology*, p. 550.

43   See John Dillenberger and Claude Welch, *Protestant Christianity: Interpreted Through its Development* (New York: Charles Scribners' Sons, 1955), p. 318 n.6.

44   Moltmann, *Theology of Hope*, p. 319.

45   George, *Theology of the Reformers*, p. 46.

46   Advisably the two works ought not to be separated simply because Alves' sacramental theology flows into his spirituality. In liberationist terms the spirituality holds all his theology together. Spirituality is Christian existence.

47   Alves writes: "It is inevitable that the community of faith and the existing order are on a collision course. Persecutions will come." Alves, *Tomorrow's Child*, p. 204

48   Alves, *Tomorrow's Child*, p. 110.

49   Alves, *ibid.*, p. 120.

50   *Ibid.*

51   Alves, *The Resurrection of the Body*, p. 58.

52   Alves, *Tomorrow's Child*, p. 71.

53   Segundo, *Sacraments Today*, p. 45.

54   Segundo, *The Community Called Church*, p. 68.

55   *Ibid.*

56   Segundo, *The Community Called Church*, p. 68.

57   *Ibid.*

58   Segundo, *Christ of the Ignatian Exercises*, p. 11.

59   Segundo, "The Option for the Poor," in *Signs of the Times*, ed. Hennelly, p. 122.

60   Segundo, The Christ of the Ignatian Exercises, p. 91.

61   Segundo, *ibid.*, pp. 137–38 n.80.

62   Segundo, *ibid.*, p. 91.

63   *Ibid.* Segundo's italics.

Conclusion

There was little doubt, as George Lindbeck maintained in his 1970 article "The Future of the Dialogue: Pluralism of an Eventual Synthesis of Doctrine," that less than a decade after the promulgation of Vatican II's decree *Unitatis Redintegratio*, the ecumenical moment generally had lost its earlier post-conciliar momentum. "I find myself agreeing," Lindbeck wrote, "that the dialogue is of little current significance either to the organized churches or to movements of renewal . . . The *avant garde* activists and theological progressives are even less concerned."[1] Thirty years after *Unitatis Redintegratio*, the movement, one may say, still lacks momentum at the level of interest in dialogue or agreements reached between the churches. Other ecumenical forms have meanwhile arisen, "secular ecumenism," as Robert Wuthnow describes it, uniting believers of different communions around positions on pressing socio-moral problems.[2]

In an earlier essay, in 1966, "The Framework of Catholic-Protestant Disagreement," Lindbeck, however, noted a development that provided a different perspective on the state of ecumenism in the churches. The common theological framework, he observed, which supported the disagreements of the sixteenth- century was in the process of changing. "All of us, Protestants and Roman Catholics alike increasingly experience and interpret both natural and supernatural realities in categories very different from those of the past."[3]

Some of the theological areas of developing agreement Lindbeck pointed to were the following: the Catholic use of "*sola scriptura*" ("*in ore ecclesiae*"); the Protestant endorsement of "*sola traditione;*" unity around the notion/reality of "*ecclesia semper reformanda*." Disagreements remained "on a relatively small number of points," Catholics, for example, affirming a certain kind of magisterial authority which Protestants exclude. Perhaps, Lindbeck added prudently, the foregoing positions were confined to persons whose "entire thinking" was shaped by the ecumenical dialogue, but the possibility of a continuance and development of the trend seemed very likely.

One may still find in the churches disagreements on different points, but at the theological level systems of thought are more and more similarly structured among Roman Catholics and Protestants, as indeed this study has shown. Despite difference in style, theme, and personal vocabulary, Segundo and Alves are excellent examples of the growing rapprochement that describes the theological enterprise.

Some key conceptual shifts, noted in the course of the study, lie behind this rapprochement. First, the static, classical two-tiered universe/ world picture has all but disappeared. What has replaced it is a picture of the world as a unified, developing, evolutionary process. The process is not necessarily regarded with the optimism of nineteenth century Liberal Theology, but it is in large part the basis for our *de facto* historical consciousness, and the futuristic shape of contemporary thinking and concern.

The theological implications of the shift in the world picture have been enormous. The sphere that transcends the reality we experience is no longer conceived of a realm of timeless truth and value above us. What transcends our experience lies instead ahead, as open possibilities in the future for liberation or bondage. Transcendence in other words is no longer encountered as discontinuous with the world, something to be entered into by escaping into eternity, but a sphere to be met as the future, continuous with, at the same time radically different from our present world.

This historical-eschatological view of transcendence constitutes a dominant overarching perspective in contemporary theology, manifestly the case in all Liberation Theology, Roman Catholic and Protestant. From this framework is generated a unified theology of grace; salvation is no longer seen as discontinuous with historical existence. It constitutes the passage from an old to a coming age, from conditions of dehumanization and bondage to conditions of maturity and freedom for the children of God. History (and sociology) have also rendered theology far more conscious of human sociality. Thus salvation can no longer be construed in terms of the individualism to which it had for centuries been tied. The human vocation is, as Liberation Theology insists, essentially a convocation.

The shifts have influenced and shaped not only theology (including ecclesiology) but modes of liturgy and piety. Sacramentology, as we saw, has been seen by liberationists as requiring an active, committed, not rote or magical, participation, and as making for real transformation, both personally and socially. The spiritual life is not a life of "eternal" concerns as opposed to less valuable, less important "temporal" ones, but a real, unified commitment, an integral way of being and doing.

Liberation Theology, Roman Catholic and Protestant, constitutes, as this study has shown theological justification for the view of incompatibility that has long defined the way the theologies of the two communions have been seen.

The clear ecumenical trajectory in Liberation Theology is of vital importance as a bridge to help the contemporary church, religious traditions, persons of goodwill and humankind as a whole to transcend the struggle for community building. The alternative is chaos. Amplification of the various dimensions of the ecumenical trajectory in Liberation Theology lie well beyond the scope of this study. Some features of future amplification can still, however, be sketched.

It is clear that the Christian tradition has little choice but to follow even further the imperative of a liberation ecumenicity. This will lead to possible dialogue among persons of the various world religious traditions. Such dialogue will provide a basis for understanding the tremendous unrest and the deep spiritual hunger and search, which are widespread among contemporary humankind. It will also provide momentum for initiatives internal and external to the churches for the unity and healing of our fragmented world.

With the dawn of the twenty-first century, Liberation Theology has already provided a meaningful lens through which the historical configurations of the coming millennium can be envisioned and evaluated. The four dimensions explored in this study, grace, faith, ecclesiology, and sacraments (including spirituality) constitute areas within which may be found indices of and directions for personal and social transformation. Liberating grace will provide empowerment for creating a compassionate future in which there will be access to a meaningful life, and where solutions to divisive human conflicts can be pursued and accomplished. Liberating faith will challenge apathy, fatalism, despair, and indifference in the face of stubborn historical problems. Going beyond a narrow individualism, such faith will lead to a renewal of the roots of human community and sociality. A liberating ecclesiology will underlie the re-structuring of public institutions, and the creation of new structures designed to promote wider human flourishing and enhancement. A liberating sacramentology will bridge the divorce between faith and life and give concrete form to a vision of integral existence for all human beings.

One must, of course, be realistic and cautionary in the midst of this optimism. Perhaps one of the greatest challenges facing liberation ecumenism is its possible captivity resulting from assimilation into mainline Roman Catholic-Protestant academic theological discourse. It is critical that this theology, in fidelity to its originating insights, remain in constant dialogue with those on the underside of history, whose voicelessness it has championed, and to whom it owes its very existence. Too often intellectual traditions and domains of discussion focus on key figures and key currents rather than the masses of ordinary people who seek a better life and a better way experiencing the world. Liberation ecumenism must resist this respectable enslavement, and not lose its capacity for deep engagement with its roots, namely, with the fears, conflicts, and hopes of human beings everywhere.

Notes

1   See George Lindbeck, "The Future of the Dialogue: Pluralism or an Eventual Synthesis of Doctrine," in Joseph Papin, ed., *Christian Action and Openness to the World* (Pennsylvania: The Villanova Press, 1970), pp. 38–39.

2   See Robert Wuthnow, *The Restructuring of American Religion: Society and Faith Since World War II* (New Jersey: Princeton University Press, 1988), p. 112, 121–131.

3   See in T. Patrick Burke, *The Word in History: The St. Xavier Symposium,* (New York: Sheed and Ward), p. 102.

Selected Bibliography

Primary Sources: Juan Luis Segundo

1. Books

————. *Berdiaeff: Une réflexion chrétienne sur la personne.* Paris: Montaigne, 1963.

————. *The Christ of the Ignatian Exercises.* Trans. John Drury. Maryknoll, NY: Orbis, 1987.

————. *The Community Called Church.* Trans. John Drury. Maryknoll, NY: Orbis, 1973.

————. *Concepción christiana del hombre.* Montevideo Mimeo-grafica "Luz", 1964.

————. *Etapas precristianos de la fe: Evolución de la idea de Dios en el Antiguo Testamento.* Montevideo: Cursos de Complementación Cristiana, 1962.

————. *Evolution and Guilt.* Trans. John Drury. Maryknoll, NY: Orbis, 1974.

————. *An Evolutionary Approach to Jesus of Nazareth.* Trans. John Drury. Maryknoll, NY: Orbis, 1988.

————. *Faith and Ideologies.* Trans. John Drury. Maryknoll, NY: Orbis/London: Sheed and Ward/Melbourne: Collins Dove, 1984.

————. *Función de la Iglesia en la realidad Rioplatense.* Montevideo: Barreriro y Ramos, 1962.

————. *Grace and the Human Condition.* Trans. John Drury. Maryknoll, NY: Orbis, 1973.

———. *The Hidden Motives of Pastoral Action: Latin American Reflections.* Trans. John Drury. Maryknoll, NY: Orbis, 1978.

———. *The Historical Jesus of the Synoptics.* Trans. John Drury. Maryknoll, NY: Orbis/London: Sheed and Ward/Melbourne: Collins Dove, 1985.

———. *El Hombre De Hoy Ante Jesus De Nazareth. Tomo I: Fe e Ideologia.* Madrid, Huesca 30–32: Ediciones Cristianidad, S. L., 1982.

———. *El Hombre De Hoy Ante De Jesus De Nazareth. Tomo II/1: Historia y Actualidad, Sinópticos y Pablo.* Madrid, Huesca 30–32: Ediciones Cristianidad, S. L., 1982.

———. *El Hombre De Hoy Ante De Jesus De Nazareth. Tomo II/2: Historia y Actualidad Las Cristologias en la Spiritualidad.* Madrid, Huesca 30–32: Ediciones Cristianidad, S. L., 1982.

———. *The Humanist Christology of Paul.* Trans. John Drury. Maryknoll, NY: Orbis/London: Sheed and Ward, 1986.

———. *¿Infierno: Futuro o presente?* Pocitos: Unpublished mimeographed transcript, Parish of Juan Bautisto, 1983.

———. *The Liberation of Dogma: Faith, Revelation, and Dogmatic Teaching Authority.* Trans. Phillip Berryman. Maryknoll, NY: Orbis, 1992.

———. *The Liberation of Theology.* Trans. John Drury. Maryknoll, NY: Orbis, 1976.

———. *Masas y minorías en la dialéctica divina de la liberación.* Buenos Aires: La Aurora, 1973

———. *Our Idea of God.* Trans. John Drury. Maryknoll, NY: Orbis, 1973.

———. *¿Que es un cristiano?* Montevideo: Mosca Hermanos S.A. Editiones, 1971.

———. *The Sacraments Today.* Trans. John Drury. Maryknoll, NY: Orbis, 1974.

———. *Signs of the Times: Theological Reflections.* Ed. Alfred T. Hennelly, S.J. Trans. Robert R. Barr. Maryknoll, NY: Orbis, 1993.

————. *Teologia Abierta I: Iglesia-Gracia.* Madrid, Huesca 30-32: Ediciones Cristianidad, S. L., 1983.

————. *Teologia Abierta II: Dios, Sacramentos, Culpa.* Madrid, Huesca 30–32: Ediciones Cristianidad, S. L., 1983.

————. *Teologia Abierta III: Reflexiones Criticas.* Madrid, Huesca 30–32: Ediciones Cristianidad, S. L., 1984.

————. *Theology and the Church: A Response to Cardinal Ratzinger and a Warning to the Whole Church.* Trans. John W. Dierckmeier. San Francisco: Harper, 1987.

2. Articles

————. "America Hoy." *Véspera* 1.2 (October, 1967): 53–57.

————. "Camilio Torres, sacerdocio y violencia." *Véspera* 1.1 (May, 1967): 71–75.

————. "Christianity and Violence in Latin America." *Christianity and Crisis* (March 4, 1968): 31–34.

————. "The Church: A New Direction in Latin America." *Catholic Mind* (March, 1967): 43–47.

————. "La condición humana." *Perspectivas de Diàlogo* 2.12 (March-April, 1967): 30–35.

————. "Condicionamientos actuales de la reflexión teologica en latinoamérica." Ed. Enrique Ruiz Maldonado. *Liberación y Cautiverio: debates en torno al método de la teología en America Latina.* Mexico City: Comite Organizador, (1975): 91–101.

————. "Conversión y reconciliación en la perspectiva de la moderna teología de la liberación." *Cristianismo y Sociedad* 13 (1975): 17–25.

————. "Derechos humanos, evangelización e ideología." *Christus* (November, 1978): 29–35.

————. "La dialectica del miedo." *Perspectivas de Diàlogo* 2.17 (September, 1967): 168–177.

————. "El diàlogo Iglesia-mundo." *Diàlogo* 1:9 (November, 1966): 5–22.

————. "El diàlogo Iglesia-mundo: reflexión." *Diàlogo* 1.6 (October, 1966): 3–7.

————. "¿Un Dios a nuestra imagen?" *Perspectivas de Diàlogo* 4.32 (March, 1969): 14–18.

————. "Education, Communication and Liberation: A Christian Vision." *IDOC International North American Edition* (November 13, 1971): 63–96

————. "Evangelización y humanización: Progreso del reino y progreso temporal." *Perspectivos de Diàlogo* 5.41 (March, 1970):9–17.

————. "Fe e ideología." *Perspectivas de Diàlogo* 9.89–90 (December, 1974): 227–233.

————. "La función de la Iglesia." *Diàlogo* 1.1 (December, 1965): 4–7; I.2 (February, 1966): 5–10; I.3 (April, 1966): 3–10.

————. "The Future of Christianity in Latin America." *Cross Currents* 12 (1963): 273–81.

————. "¿Hacia una Iglesia de izquierda?" *Perspectivas de Diàlogo* 4.32 (April, 1969): 35–39.

————. "La ideología de un diario católico." *Perspectivas de Diàlogo* 5.44–45 (June–July, 1970): 136–144.

————. "La Iglesia chilena ante el socialismo I." *Marcha* 1558 (August 27, 1971).

————. "La iglesia chilena ante el socialismo II." *Marcha* 1559 (September 4, 1971):

————. "La iglesia chilena ante el socialismo III." *Marcha* 1560 (September 11, 1971).

————. "¿La iglesia es necessaria?" *Diàlogo* 1.7 (September, 1966): 3–8.

————. "Introduction." *Iglesia latinoamericana ¿Protesta o Pro-fecia?* Buenos Aires: Ediciones Busqueda, 1969: 8–17.

————. "Liberación: Fe e ideología." *Mensaje* (July, 1972): 248–254.

————. "Lo que el concilio dice." *Diàlogo* 1.10 (December, 1966): 3–13.

————. "On a Missionary Awareness of One's Own Culture." *Studies in the International Apostolate of Jesuits* 33.1 (1974): 33–47.

————. "Padre, Hijo, Espiritu: Una Historia. *Perspectivas de Diàlogo* 3.23 (July, 1968): 71–76.

————. "Padre, Hijo, Espiritu: Una sociedad." *Perspectivas de Diàlogo* 3.24 (July, 1968): 103–109.

————. "Padre, Hijo, Espiritu: Una libertad I." *Perspectivas de Diàlogo* 3.25 (July, 1968): 142–148.

————. "Padre, Hijo, Espiritu: Una libertad II." *Perspectivas de Diàlogo* 3.25 (August, 1968): 183–186.

————. "Perspectivas para una teología latinoamericana." *Perspectivas de Diàlogo* 9.17 (1977): 9–25.

————. "The Possible Contribution of Protestant Theology to Latin American Christianity in the Future." *The Lutheran Quarterly* 22 (Fall, 1970): 60–67.

————. "Profundidad de la gracia." *Perspectivas de Diàlogo* 2.19 (November, 1967): 235–240; III.20 (December, 1967): 249–255.

————. "¿Qué nombre dar a la existencia cristiana?" *Perspectivas de Diàlogo* 2.11 (January-February, 1967): 3–9.

————. "Revelación, fe, signos de los tiempos." *Revista latinoamericana de Teología* 5.4 (May-August, 1988): 123–144.

————. "Ritmos de cambio y pastoral de conjunto." *Perspectivas de Diàlogo* 4.35 (July, 1969): 131–137.

————. "Social Justice and Revolution." *America* 118 (April 27, 1968): 574–577.

————. "Teología: Mensaje y proceso." *Perspectivas de Diàlogo* 9.89–90 (December, 1974): 259–270.

————. "Two Theologies of Liberation." *The Month* 17 (October, 1984): 321–327.

————. "La vida eterna." *Perspectivas de Diàlogo* 2.14 (June, 1967): 83–89; 2.15 (July, 1967): 109–118.

————. "Wealth and Poverty as Obstacles to Development." In *Human Rights and the Liberation of Man in the Americas.* Ed. Louis Colonnesse. South Bend, IN: U Notre Dame P (1971): 23–31.

Secondary Sources: Juan Luis Segundo

1. Books

Hennelly, Alfred T. *Theologies in Conflict: The Challenge of Juan Luis Segundo.* Maryknoll, NY: Orbis, 1979.

Lowe Ching, Theresa. *Efficacious Love: Its Meaning and Function in the Theology of Juan Luis Segundo.* Lanham, MD: UP America, 1989.

Nealen, Mary Kaye. *The Poor in the Ecclesiology of Juan Luis Segundo.* New York, et al: Peter Lang, 1991.

Persha, Gerald J. *Juan Luis Segundo: A Study Concerning the Relationship between the Particularity of the Church and the Universality of Her Mission.* Maryknoll, NY: Orbis, 1980.

Slade, Stanley David. *The Theological Method of Juan Luis Segundo.* Diss. Fuller Theological Seminary, 1979.

2. Articles

Baum, Gregory. "Theological Method of Segundo's *The Liberation of Theology.*"*CTSA Proceedings* 32 (1977): 120–124.

Cabestrero, Teófilo. "A Conversation with Juan Luis Segundo, S.J." In Ed. Teófilo Cabestrero. *Faith: Conversations with Contemporary Theologians.* Trans. Donald D. Walsh. Maryknoll, NY: Orbis (1980): 172–180.

Hennelly, Alfred T. "The Challenge of Juan Luis Segundo." *Theological Studies* 38 (1977): 125–135.

Sanks, T. Howland, and B. Smith. "Liberation Ecclesiology: Praxis, Theory, Praxis." *Theological Studies* 38 (1977): 3–38.

Stefano, Frances. "The Evolutionary Categories of Juan Luis Segundo's Theology of Grace," *Horizons* 19.1 (1992): 7–30.

Primary Sources: Rubem A. Alves

1. Books

———. *A Selva e o Mar. Una Historia de un Amor Que Foi.* São Paulo: Paulinas, 1987.

———. *Conversas Com Quem Gostas de Ensinar.* São Paulo: Cortez Editora and Editores Associados, 1984.

————. *Da Esperanáa.* Translated from English by Joao Francisco Duarte, Jr. Campinas: Papirus, 1987.

————. *Dogmatismo e Tolerència.* São Paulo: Paulinas, 1982.

————. *Estorias de Quem Gosta de Ensinar,* 4th Edition. São Paulo: Cortez Editora and Editores Associados, 1985.

————. *Filosofia da Ciància. Introduá o ao Jogo e suas Regras,* 6th Edition. São Paulo: Brasiliense, 1985.

————. *Gandhi. A Politica dos Gestos Poeticos.* São Paulo: Brasiliense, 1983.

————. *I Believe in the Resurrection of the Body.* Minneapolis: Fortress Press, 1986.

————. *O Enigma da Religio,* 3rd Edition. São Paulo: Papirus. 1984.

————. *O Suspiro dos Oprimidos.* São Paulo: CEID and Paulinas, 1987.

————. *Pai Nosso.* São Paulo: CEID and Paulinas, 1987.

————. *Poesia Profecia Magia.* Rio de Janeiro: CEDI, 1983.

————. *The Poet, the Warrior, the Prophet.* London and Philadelphia: SCM and TPI, 1990.

————. *Protestantism and Repression: A Brazilian Case Study.* Trans. John Drury. Maryknoll, NY: Orbis, 1985.

————. *Religion: Opio o instrumento del liberación?* Translated from the English by Rosario Torrente with a Prologue by José Míguez Bonino. Montevideo: Tierra Nueva, 1970.

————. *Towards A Theology of Liberation: An Exploration of the Encounter between the Languages of Humanistic Messianism and Messianic Humanism.* Diss.: Princeton, 1968. Theological Seminary, 1968.

————. *A Theology of Human Hope.* Washington: Corpus, 1969.

————. *Tomorrow's Child: Imagination, Creativity and the Rebirth of Culture.* New York: Harper, 1972.

————. *Variaá es Sobre a Vida e a Morte.* São Paulo: Paulinas, 1982.

————. *What is Religion?.* Trans. Don Vinzant. Maryknoll, NY: Orbis, 1984.

2. Articles

————. "Apuntes para un programa de reconstruccion en la Teologia." *Cristianis mo y Sociedad* 9.21 (1969): 21–31.

————. "Biblical Faith and the Poor of the World." Ed. R. Shinn. *Faith and Science in an Unjust World* (1980): 373–375.

————. "Blessed Are the Hungry: An Advent Meditation for Vancouver on Hunger and Life." Trans. A. Sapsezian. *The Ecumenical Review* 35 (July, 1983): 239–245.

————. "Carta de Rubem Alves." *Cristianismo y Sociedad* 21.1 (1983): 63–64.

————. "Carta de Rubem Alves." *Cristianismo y Sociedad* 75 (Primera entrega) (1983): 63.

————. "The Case Against the New Roman Catholic Spirituality." *Paul VI: Critical Appraisals.* Ed. J. F. Andrews, (1970): 41–60.

————. "Christian Realism: Ideology of the Establishment." *Christianity and Crisis* 33 (September 17, 1973): 173–176.

————. "From Paradise to the Desert: Autobiographical Musings." Trans. John Drury. *Frontiers of Theology in Latin America.* Ed. Rosino Gibellini. Maryknoll, NY: Orbis (1979): 284–303.

————. "God's People and Man's Liberation." *Communio Viatorium* 14.2–3 (1971): 107–115.

————. "Human Values: The Crisis in the Congregation." *International Review of Missions* 60.237 (January, 1971): 70–80.

————. "Injustice and Revolt." Address given at the Nineteenth Ecumenical Student Conference on the Christian World Mission at Ohio University, Athens, OH. New York: National Student Christian Federation (1964).

————. "Injusticia y rebelión." *Cristianismo y Sociedad* 2.6 (1964): 40–53.

————. "An Invitation to Dream." *The Ecumenical Review* 39 (January, 1987): 59–62.

————. "Is there any Future for Protestantism in Latin America?" *The Lutheran Quarterly* 22.1 (1970): 49–50.

————. "Latin American Protestantism: Utopia Becomes Ideology." *Our Claim On the Future*. Ed. Jorge Lara-Braud, (Friendship Press, 1970): 62–78.

————. "Latin American Protestantism: Utopia Becomes Ideology." In revised form as: "Protestantism in Latin America: Its Ideological Function and Utopian Possibilities." *The Ecumenical Review* 22.1 (January, 1970): 1–15.

————. "Magic and Theory." *Christianity and Crisis* 31:8 (May, 1971): 110–111.

————. "Marxism as the Guarantee of Faith." *Worldview* 16 (March, 1973): 13–17.

————. "El Milagro inesperado." *Significado Sociopolitico-religioso de la visita de Juan Pablo II a America Latina Cuadernos Cristianismo Soc.* 6.38 (November, 1981): 1–63.

————. "El ministerio social de la iglesia local." ISAL (Cristianismo y Sociedad) *La Responsabilidad Social del Cristiano* (1964): 56–65.

————. "La muerte de la iglesia y el futuro del hombre." *Cristianismo y Sociedad* 6.16–17 (1968): 3–10.

————. "Personal Wholeness and Political Creativity: The Theology of Liberation and Pastoral Care." *Pastoral Psychology* 26 (Winter, 1977): 124–136.

————. "Play or How To Subvert Dominant Values." *Union Seminary Quarterly* 26.1 (Fall, 1970): 43–57.

————. "Priorities for Peace in Inter-American Relations." *World Christian Education* Second and Third Quarters (1967): 40–44.

————. "Priorities for Peace in Inter-American Relations." Study document prepared at the request of the Commission on Ecumenical Mission and Relations of the United Presbyterian Church in the U.S.A. (1966).

————. "El pueblo de Dios y la búsqueda de un nuevo orden social." *Cristianismo y Sociedad* 9.26–27 (1971): 5–27.

————. "El pueblo de Dios y la liberación del hombre." Teología de la liberación. ISAL, ed. *Cristianismo y Sociedad* (1970): 7–12.

————. "Religion: Pathology or Search for Sanity?" Trans. D. C. Hoffman. Indianapolis: *Encounter* 36 (Winter, 1975): 1–9.

————. "Le Retour du sacré: les chemins de la sociologie de la religion au Brésil." Trans. C. Beylier. *Archives de Sciences Sociales des Religions* 47.1 (January-March, 1979): 23–51.

————. "Rubem Alves. An interview with Elsa Támez." *Against Machismo.* Ed. Elsa Támez. Oak Park, IL: Meyer-Stone (1987): 68–75.

————. "Sobre la vida de las iglesias y el movimiento ecumenico en America Latina: Una posición de ISAL." *Cristianismo y Sociedad* 7.19 (1969): issue 2, 5–15.

————. "Some Thoughts on a Program for Ethics." *Union Seminary Quarterly Review* 26.2 (Winter, 1971): 153–170.

————. "Sometimes." *Union Seminary Quarterly Review* 40.3 (1985): 43–53.

————. "Theology and the Liberation of Man." *In Search of a Theology of Development.* Ed. Gerhard Bauer, SODEPAX (1970): 75–92.

————. "Theology and the Liberation of Man." *New Theology* 9. Eds. Martin Marty, Dean G. Peerman, New York: Macmillan (1972): 230–250.

————. "Theopoetics: Longing and Liberation." *Struggles for Solidarity: Liberation Theologies in Tension.* Eds. Lorine M. Getz, Ruy O. Costa, Minneapolis: Fortress (1992): 159–171.

————. "Variations on the Theme of Reconciliation." *Reformed World* 38.4 (1984): 240–246.

————. "Violence and Counterviolence." *Cultural Factors in Inter-American Relations.* Ed. Samuel Shapiro, (Notre Dame/ London: University of Notre Dame Press, 1968): 35–38.

————. "What Does It Mean to Say the Truth?" *Sciences and Theology in the Twentieth Century.* Ed. A. Peacocke, (1981): 163–181.

————. "'Where Is the Church?' Giving Account of Faith: Political and Social Implications." *St Enc* 11:2 (1975): 1–16.

Secondary Sources: Rubem A. Alves

1. Books

Costa, Ruy Otavio. *Toward a Latin American Protestant Ethic of Liberation: A Comparative Study of the Writings of Rubem Alves* and José Míguez-Bonino from the Perspective of the Sources and Substance of their Social Ethics. Diss. Boston U., 1990.

Meeks, M. Douglas. Origins of the Theology of Hope. Philadelphia: Fortress, 1974.

Schubeck, Thomas Louis. Liberation and Imagination: A New Theological Language in Response to the Marxist Critique of Religion. Diss. U. Southern Cal., 1975.

Zike, Allen Douglas. Transcendence: The Difference Between Secular and Christian Liberation as Seen in Pedagogy of the Oppressed by Paulo Freire and A Theology of Human Hope by Rubem Alves. Diss. Saint Louis U, 1983.

2. Articles

Kollar, Nathan R. "Exploring the Nature of Religious Belief." Books and Religion 13.1 (1985): 6.

Melano Couch, Beatriz. "New Visions of the Church in Latin America: A Protestant View." The Emergent Gospel. Eds. Sergio Torres, Virginia Fabella. Maryknoll, NY: Orbis, 1978.

Moltmann, Jürgen. "A Theology of Liberation." Compass Theology Review 7:1. (1973): 12–17.

Selected Books and Articles Related to this Study

1. Books

Andrews, James F., ed. Paul VI: Critical Appraisals. New York/ London: Bruce Pub. Co./Collier Macmillan Ltd., 1970.

Araya, Victorio. God of the Poor: The Mystery of God in Latin American Liberation Theology. Trans. Robert R. Barr. Maryknoll, NY: Orbis, 1987.

Assmann, Hugo. Opresion-Liberacion: Desafio a los Cristianos. Montevideo, Uruguay: Tierra Nueva, 1971.

———. Theology for a Nomad Church. Trans. Paul Burns. Maryknoll, NY: Orbis, 1976.

Balasuriya, Tissa. Planetary Theology. Maryknoll, NY: Orbis, 1984.

Bateson, Gregory. Mind and Nature: A Necessary Unity. New York: Bantam, 1979.

———. Steps to an Ecology of Mind. New York: Ballantine, 1972.

Bauckham, Richard J. *Moltmann: Messianic Theology in the Making.* Southampton, UK: Marshall Pickering, 1987.

Bauer, Gerhard, ed. *In Search of a Theology of Development: Papers from a Consultation on Theology and Development held by SODEPAX in Cartigny, Switzerland, November, 1969.* Geneva: Committee on Society, Development and Peace, 1969.

Baum, Gregory. *Man Becoming: God in Secular Experience.* New York: Herder, 1971.

————. *Religion and Alienation: A Theological Reading of Sociology.* New York: Paulist, 1975.

Biéler, André. *The Social Humanism of Calvin.* Trans. Paul T. Fuhrmann. Richmond, Virginia: The John Knox Press, 1964.

Blondel, Maurice. *Action: Essay on a Critique of Life and a Science of Practice.* Trans. of *L'Action. Essai d'une critique de la vie et d'une science de la practique.* Trans. Oliva Blanchette. Notre Dame: U Notre Dame P, 1984.

Boff, Clodovis and Boff, Leonardo. *Introducing Liberation Theology.* Trans. Paul Burns. Maryknoll: NY: Orbis, 1987.

Boff, Clodovis. *Theology and Praxis: Epistemological Foundations.* Trans. Robert R. Barr. Maryknoll, NY: Orbis, 1987.

Boff, Leonardo. *Church: Charism and Power: Liberation Theology and the Institutional Church.* New York: Crossroad, 1986.

————. *Liberating Grace.* Trans. John Drury. Maryknoll, NY: Orbis, 1979.

Bonhoeffer, Dietrich. *The Cost of Discipleship.* Revised Edition. New York: Macmillan, 1963.

Burke, T. Patrick, ed. *The Word in History: The St. Xavier Symposium.* New York: Sheed and Ward, 1966.

Cabestrero, Teófilo, ed. *Faith: Conversations with Contemporary Theologians.* Trans. Donald D. Walsh. Maryknoll, NY: Orbis, 1980.

Calvin, John. *Calvin: Institutes of the Christian Religion. Vol. 1.* Ed. John T. McNeil, Trans. Ford Lewis Battles. Library of Christian Classics, Vol. XX: Book I.i To III.xix. Philadelphia: The Westminster Press, 1960.

————. *Calvin: Institutes of the Christian Religion. Vol. 2.* Ed. John T. McNeil, Trans. Ford Lewis Battles. Library of Christian Classics, Vol. XXI: Books III. XX To IV.XX. Philadelphia: The Westminster Press, 1960.

————. *Selections from His Writings.* Ed. John Dillenberger. New York: Anchor Books, Doubleday, 1971.

Comblin, José. *The Holy Spirit and Liberation.* Trans. Paul Burns. Maryknoll, NY: Orbis, 1979.

Cox, Harvey. *The Silencing of Leonardo Boff.* Oak Park, IL: Meyer Stone, 1988.

Dillenberger, John and Claude Welsh. *Protestant Christianity: Interpreted Through its Development.* New York: Charles Scribners' Sons, 1955.

Dussell, Enrique. *Philosophy of Liberation.* Trans. Aquilina Martinez and Christine Markovsky. Maryknoll, NY: Orbis, 1985.

Ebeling, Gerhard. *The Nature of Faith.* Trans. Ronald Gregor Smith. Philadelphia: Fortress Press, 1967.

Ellacuría, Ignacio and Jon Sobrino, eds. *Mysterium Liberationis: Conceptos Fundamentales de la Teología de la Liberación, I, II.* Madrid: Editorial Trotta, S. A., 1992.

Ellis, H. and Otto Maduro, eds. *The Future of Liberation Theology: Essays in Honor of Gustavo Gutiérrez.* Maryknoll, NY: Orbis, 1989.

Fabella, Virginia and Sergio Torres, eds. *Doing Theology in a Divided World. Papers from the Sixth International Conference of the Ecumenical Association of Third World Theologians, January 5–13, 1983, Geneva, Switzerland.* Maryknoll, NY: Orbis, 1985.

Ferm, Deane William. *Third World Liberation Theologies: An Introductory Survey.* Maryknoll, NY: Orbis, 1986.

Flannery, Austin, ed. *Vatican Council II: The Conciliar and Post-Conciliar Documents.* Fifth Printing. Collegeville, MN: Liturgical Press, 1980.

Freire, Paulo. *Pedagogy of the Oppressed.* Trans. Myra Bergman Ramos. New York: Continuum, 1992.

Gaines, David P. *The World Council of Churches: A Study of Its Background and History.* Peterborough, New Hampshire: Richard R. Smith, Noone House, 1966.

George, Timothy. *Theology of the Reformers*. Nashville, TN: Broadman Press, 1988.

Getz, Lorine M. and Ruy O. Costa, eds. *Struggles for Solidarity: Liberation Theologies in Tension*. Minneapolis: Fortress, 1992.

Gibellini, Rosino, ed. *Frontiers of Theology in Latin America*. Maryknoll, NY: Orbis, 1979.

Gilkey, Langdon. *Society and the Sacred: Toward a Theology of Culture in Decline*. New York: Crossroads, 1981.

Gottwald, Norman K., ed. *The Bible and Liberation: Political and Social Hermeneutics*. Maryknoll, NY: Orbis, 1983.

de Gruchy, John W. *Liberating Reformed Theology: A South African Contribution to an Ecumenical Debate*. Grand Rapids, Michigan: William B. Eerdmans/Cape Town: David Philip, 1991.

Gutiérrez, Gustavo. *A Theology of Liberation: History, Politics and Salvation*. Trans. and Ed. Sr. Caridad Inda and John Eagleson, 15th Anniversary Edition. Maryknoll, NY: Orbis, 1988.

———. *The Power of the Poor in History*. Trans. Robert R. Barr. Maryknoll, NY: Orbis, 1983.

———. *The Truth Shall Make You Free: Confrontations*. Maryknoll, NY: Orbis, 1990.

Haight, Roger. *An Alternative Vision: An Interpretation of Liberation Theology*. New York: Paulist, 1985.

Harvey, Van A. *A Handbook of Theological Terms*. New York: Collier Books, London: Collier Macmillan, 1964.

Hassett, John and Lacey, Hugh, eds. *Towards a Society That Serves Its People: The Intellectual Contribution of El Salvador's Murdered Jesuits*. Washington, DC: Georgetown University Press, 1991.

Hastings, Adrian, ed. *Modern Catholicism: Vatican II and After*. Adrian Hastings, ed. London and New York: SPCK and Oxford UP, 1991.

Hennelly, Alfred T., ed. *Liberation Theology: A Documentary History*. Maryknoll, NY: Orbis, 1990.

Hôpfl, Haro. *The Christian Polity of John Calvin*. Cambridge: Cambridge University Press, 1992.

Kaufmann, Walter, ed. *Religion from Tolstoy to Camus*. New York: Harper & Brothers, 1961.

Kee, Alistair. *Marx and the Failure of Liberation Theology*. London: SCM, Philadelphia: Trinity Press International, 1991.

Küng, Hans and David Tracy, eds. *Paradigm Change in Theology: A Symposium for the Future*. Trans. Margaret Kôhl. New York: Crossroad, 1989.

Küng, Hans. *Justification: The Doctrine of Karl Barth and a Catholic Reflection*. Philadelphia: The Westminster Press, 1981.

Lakeland, Paul. *Theology and Critical Theory: Discourse of the Church*. Nashville: Abingdon Press, 1990.

Lamb, Matthew L. *Solidarity with Victims: Towards a Theology of Social Transformation*. New York: Crossroad, 1982.

Lara-Braud, Jorge, ed. *Our Claim On the Future*. New York: Friendship Press, 1970.

Lehmann, Karl and Wolfhart Pannenberg, eds. *The Condemnations of the Reformation Era: Do They Still Divide?* Trans. Margaret Kôhl. Minneapolis: Fortress Press, 1990.

Lehmann, Paul. *Ideology and Incarnation*. Geneva: John Knox Press, 1962.

————. *Ethics in a Christian Context*. New York and Evanston: Harper, 1963.

Lobkowics, Nicholas. *Theory and Practice: History of a Concept from Aristotle to Marx*. Notre Dame and London: U Notre Dame Press, 1967.

de Lubac, Henri. *The Mystery of the Supernatural*. Trans. Rosemary Sheed. New York: Herder & Herder, 1965.

Luther, Martin. *Martin Luther's Basic Theological Writings*. Ed. Timothy F. Lull. Minneapolis: Fortress, 1989.

————. *Three Treatises*. Philadelphia: Fortress Press, 1960.

Lyons, James A. *The Cosmic Christ in Origen and Teilhard de Chardin: A Comparative Study*. New York: Oxford University Press, 1982.

Macquarrie, John. *Twentieth-Century Religious Thought*. London: SCM/ Philadelphia: Trinity Press International, 1989.

Machoveč, Milan. *A Marxist Looks at Jesus*. Philadelphia and London: Fortress and Darton, Longman & Todd, 1976.

Malevez, L. *Le Message Chrétien et Le Mythe: La Théologie de Rudolf Bultmann*. Bruxelles et al: Desclée de Brouwer, 1954.

Mannheim, Karl. *Ideology and Utopia: An Introduction to the Sociology of Knowledge*. Trans. Louis Wirth and Edward Shils. New York: Harcourt, 1936.

Marcel, Gabriel. Homo Viator: *Introduction to a Metaphysic of Hope*. Trans. Emma Craufurd. Chicago: Henry Regnery, 1951.

Marcuse, Herbert. *Reason and Revolution: Hegel and the Rise of Social Theory*, 2d edition. New York: Humanities Press, 1954.

Marty, Martin and Dean G. Peerman, eds. *New Theology 9*. New York: Macmillan, 1972.

Marx, Karl and Frederick Engels. *Collected Works, Vol. 5: Marx and Engels 1845–1847*. New York: International Publishers, 1975.

Meeks, M. Douglas. *Origins of the Theology of Hope*. Philadelphia: Fortress Press, 1974.

Míguez Bonino, José. *Christians and Marxists: The Mutual Challenge to Revolution*. Grand Rapids, MI: Eerdmans, 1976.

————. *Doing Theology in a Revolutionary Situation*. Philadelphia: Fortress, 1975.

Min, Anselm K. *Dialectic of Salvation: Issues in Theology of Liberation*. Albany, NY: State U of NY, 1989.

Miranda, José Porfirio. *Being and the Messiah*. Trans. John Eagleson. Maryknoll, NY: Orbis, 1974.

————. *Marx and the Bible*. Trans. John Eagleson. Maryknoll, NY: Orbis, 1974.

Moltmann, Jürgen. *The Crucified God. The Cross as the Foundation and Criticism of Christian Theology*. New York et al: Harper, 1974.

————. *Theology of Hope: On the Ground and the Implication of a Christian Eschatology*. New York: Harper, 1967.

Mozley, E. N. *The Theology of Albert Schweitzer for Christian Inquir-ers*. West Port, CT: Greenwood Press, 1974.

Neely, Alan P. *Protestant Antecedents of the Latin American Theol-ogy of Liberation*. Ann Arbor: U Microfilms, 1986.

Neuner, J. and Dupuis, J., eds. *The Christian Faith in the Documents of the Catholic Church*. Revised Edition. New York: Alba House, 1962.

Niebuhr, Reinhold. *The Nature and Destiny of Man, Vol. I, II*. New York: Scribner's, 1943.

Niesel, Wilhelm. *The Gospel and the Churches: A Comparison of Catholi-cism, Orthodoxy and Protestantism*. Trans. David Lewis. Phila-delphia: The Westminster Press, 1962.

Papin, Joséph, ed. *Christian Action and Openness to the World*. Penn-sylvania: The Villanova Press, 1970.

Peacocke, A. R., ed. *The Sciences and Theology in the Twentieth Cen-tury*. Indiana: University of Notre Dame, 1981.

Rahner, Karl. *Theological Investigations, Volume 1*. Trans. Cornelius Ernst. Baltimore: Helicon Press, 1961.

————. *Nature and Grace: Dilemmas in the Modern Church*. New York: Sheed and Ward, 1964.

————. *Foundations of the Christian Faith: An Introduction to the Idea of Christianity*. Trans. William V. Dych. New York: Cross-road, 1978.

Richardson, Alan and Bowden, John, eds. *The Westminster Dictionary of Christian Theology*. Philadelphia, Pennsylvania: The Westminster Press, 1983.

Rouse, Ruth and Neil, Stephen Charles. *A History of the Ecumenical Movement, Vol. I, 1517 1948. Third Edition*. Geneva: World Council of Churches, 1986.

Runyon, Theodore, ed. *Sanctification and Liberation: Liberation The-ology in the Light of the Wesleyan Tradition*. Nashville, TN: Abingdon Press, 1981.

Schillebeeckx, Edward. *Christ: The Experience of Jesus as Lord*. Trans. John Bowden. New York: Crossroad, 1980.

———. *Jesus: An Experiment in Christology.* Trans. Hubert Hoskins. New York: Crossroad, 1979.

Schuurman, Douglas J. *Creation, Eschaton, and Ethics: The Ethical Significance of the Creation-Eschaton Relation in the Thought of Emil Brunner and Jürgen Moltmann.* American University Studies, Series VIII Theology and Religion, Vol. 86. New York et al: Peter Lang, 1991.

Schweitzer, Albert. *The Quest of the Historical Jesus: A Critical Study of its Progress from Reimarus to Wrede.* London: T. & T. Black, 1926.

Second General Conference of Latin American Bishops (CELAM). *The Church in the Present-Day Transformation of Latin America in the Light of the Council I. Position Papers.* Bogota, Colombia, 1970.

———. *The Church in the Present-Day Transformation of Latin America in the Light of the Council II. Conclusions. Second Edition.* Bogota, Colombia: 1970.

———. *The Church in the Present-Day Transformation of Latin America in the Light of the Council. Part II: Conclusions. Third edition.* Washington, DC: NCCB, 1979.

Shapiro, Samuel, ed. *Cultural Factors in Inter-American Relations.* Notre Dame/London: University of Notre Dame Press, 1968.

Shinn, Roger L., ed. *Faith and Science in an Unjust World. Report of the World Council of Churches' Conference on Faith, Science and the Future. M.I.T. Cambridge, U.S.A. 12–24 July, 1979. Vol. 1 Plenary Presentations.* Philadelphia: Fortress Press, 1980.

Sobrino, Jon. *Christology at the Crossroads: A Latin American Approach.* Trans. John Drury. Maryknoll, NY: Orbis, 1978.

———. *Jesus in Latin America.* Maryknoll, NY: Orbis, 1987.

Stefano, Frances. *The Absolute Value of Human Action in the Theology of Juan Luis Segundo.* Lanham et al: University of America Press, 1992.

Támez, Elsa. *Amnesty of Grace: Justification by Faith from a Latin American Perspective.* Trans. Sharon H. Ringe. Nashville: Abingdon Press, 1993.

————. ed. *Against Machismo*. Oak Park, IL: Meyer-Stone, 1987.

Tillich, Paul. *The Courage to Be*. New Haven, CT: Yale UP, 1952.

————. *Dynamics of Faith*. New York: Harper/Torchbooks, 1957.

————. *The Protestant Era*. Trans. James Luther Adams. Chicago: U Chicago P, 1957.

————. *Systematic Theology, Vol. 1–3*. Chicago: U Chicago P, 1951–1963.

Torres, Sergio and John Eagleson, eds. *The Challenge of the Basic Christian Communities, Papers from the International Ecumenical Congress of Theology, February 20–March 2, 1980 São Paulo, Brazil*. Trans. John Drury. Maryknoll, NY: Orbis, 1980.

Troeltsch, Ernst. *Writings on Theology and Religion*. Trans. Robert Morgan and Michael Pye. Atlanta, GA: John Knox, 1977.

————. *The Social Teaching of the Christian Churches, Volume Two*. Trans. Olive Wyon. London: George Allen & Unwin, 1931.

United States Catholic Conference. *The Church in the Present-Day Transformation of Latin America in the Light of Vatican II*. Washington, DC: US Catholic Conference, 1973.

Visser 't Hooft, W. A., ed. *The New Delhi Report: The Third Assembly of the World Council of Churches*. London, 1962.

World Council of Churches. *Baptism, Eucharist and Ministry. Faith and Order Paper No. 111*. Geneva: WCC, 1982.

Wuthnow, Robert. *The Restructuring of American Religion: Society and Faith Since World War II*. New Jersey: Princeton UP, 1988.

Yule, George, ed. *Luther: Theologian for Catholics and Protestants*. Edinburgh: T & T. Clark, 1985.

2. Articles

Berry, Thomas. "The Place of Teilhard in The Christian Tradition." *Teilhard Perspective* 24:1 (June 1991), pp. 6–7.

Boff, Leonardo. "The Contribution of Liberation Theology to a New Paradigm." Hans Küng and Langdon Gilkey, eds. *Theology: A Symposium for the Future*. Trans. Margaret Kôhl. New York: Crossroad, 1989: 408–423.

Cerutti-Guldberg, Horace. "Actual Situation and Perspectives of Latin American Philosophy for Liberation," *The Philosophical Forum* 20:1–2 (Fall–Winter, 1988–89): 43–61.

Gutiérrez-Merino, Gustavo. "The Meaning of Development (Notes on a Theology of Liberation)." in Ed. Gerhard Bauer, *In Search of a Theology of Development*. Cartigny, Switzerland: SODEPAX (1969): 116–179.

Hanson, A. T. "Eschatology." in Eds. Alan Richardson and John Bowden. *The Westminster Dictionary of Christian Theology*. Philadelphia, Pennsylvania: The Westminster Press, 1983: 183–186.

Joint Lutheran/Roman Catholic Study Commission on "The Gospel and the Church." "The Report." *Lutheran World* XIX:1 (1972): 259–273.

Küng, Hans. "Paradigm Change in Theology." in Eds. Donald Musser and Joséph Price. *The Whirlwind in Culture, Frontiers in Theology*. Bloomington, IN: Meyer-Stone (1988): 67–105.

Lindbeck, George A. "The Framework of Catholic- Protestant Disagreement." in Ed. T. Patrick Burke. *The Word in History: The St. Xavier Symposium*. New York: Sheed & Ward (1966): 102–119.

———. "The Future of the Dialogue: Pluralism or an Eventual Synthesis of Doctrine?." in Ed. Joséph Papin. *Christian Action and Openness to the World*. Pennsylvania: Villanova UP (1970): 37–51.

———. "Interview with George Lindbeck." Ed. Patrick Granfield. *Theologians at Work*. New York & London: Macmillan (1967): 151–164.

Malevez, Leopold. "La gratuité du surnaturel." *Nouvelle Révue Théologique* 75.6 (June, 1953): 561–586.

Mertens, Herman-Emiel. Nature and Grace in Twentieth-Century Catholic Theology." *Louvain Studies* 16.3 (1991): 243–262.

Míguez Bonino, José. "A Latin American Attempt to Locate the Question of Unity." *Ecumenical Review* 26 (1974): 210–221.

———. "Wesley's Doctrine of Sanctification From a Liberationist Perspective." in Ed. Theodore Runyon. *Sanctification and Liberation: Liberation Theology in the Light of Wesleyan Tradition*. Nashville, TN: Abingdon, 1981: 49–63.

Min, Anselm K. "How Not to Do a Theology of Liberation. A Critique of Schubert Ogden," *Journal of the American Academy of Religions* 57. 1 (1989): 83–101.

Moltmann, Jürgen. "Hope." in Eds. Alan Richardson and John Bowden. *The Westminster Dictionary of Christian Theology.* Philadelphia, Pennsylvania: The Westminster Press, 1983: 270–272.

————. "An Open Letter to José Míguez Bonino (March 29, 1976). in Ed. Alfred T. Hennelly, S. J. *Liberation Theology: A Documentary History.* Maryknoll, NY: Orbis, 1990: 195–204.

Oliveros, Roberto. "Historia de la Teología de la Liberación." in Eds. Ignacio Ellacuría, Jon Sobrino. *Mysterium Liberationis: Conceptos Fundamentales de la Teología de la Liberación I, II.* Madrid: Editorial Trotta, S. A., 1992: 17–50.

Rahner, Karl. "Concerning the Relationship between Nature and Grace." *Theological Investigations 1.* Baltimore: Helicon (1961): 297–346.

————. "Nature and Grace." *Theological Investigations 4.* New York: Seabury (1974): 165–188.

Rendtorff, Trutz. "The Modern Age as a Chapter in the History of Christianity; or, The Legacy of Historical Consciousness in Present Theology." *Journal of Religion* 65.4 (1985): 478–499.

Reno, R.R. "Christology in Political and Liberation Theology." *Thomist* 56.2 (1992): 291–322.

Rupp, Gordon. "Miles Emeritus? Continuity and Discontinuity Between the Young and the Old Luther." Ed. George Yule. *Luther: Theologian for Catholics and Protestants.* Edinburgh: T. & T. Clark, 1985: 75–86.

Santa Ana, Julio. "The Influence of Bonhoeffer on the Theology of Liberation." *Ecumenical Review* 28 (1976): 189–97.

Schweitzer, Albert. "The Conception of the Kingdom of God in the Transformation of Eschatology," in Walter Kaufmann, Selected by, with an Introduction and prefaces. *Religion from Tolstoy to Camus.* New York: Harper & Brothers, 1961: 407–424.

Tavard, George. "Ecumenical Relations" in Ed. Adrian Hastings, *Modern Catholicism.* New York: Oxford University Press, 1991: 399–421.

TeSelle, Eugene. "The Problem of Nature and Grace." *Journal of Religion* 45 (1965): 238–241.

Visser 't Hooft, W. A." The Word 'Ecumenical'—Its History and Use," in Ruth Rouse, Stephen Charles Neil. *A History of the Ecumenical Movement, Vol. I, 1517–1948. Third Edition.* Geneva: World Council of Churches, 1986, pp. 735–40.

Wakefield, Gordon S. "Spirituality." in Eds. Alan Richardson and John Bowden. *The Westminster Dictionary of Christian Theology.* Philadelphia, Pennsylvania: The Westminster Press, 1983: 549–550.

Yule, George. "Introduction" Ed. George Yule. *Luther: Theologian for Catholics and Protestants.* Edinburgh: T. & T. Clark, 1985: ix–xi.

Index